LIFEWAYS

The Navajo

RAYMOND BIAL

BENCHMARK BOOKS

MARSHALL CAVENDISH
NEW YORK

SERIES CONSULTANT: JOHN BIERHORST

ACKNOWLEDGMENTS

This book would not have been possible without the generous help of a number of individuals and organizations that have dedicated themselves to preserving and advancing the culture of the Navajo people. I would like to thank the staff at the Navajo Nation tribal offices for allowing me to photograph on the Navajo Reservation. I am especially grateful to Stanley Perry, who guided me on my journey through Monument Valley, Canyon de Chelly, Window Rock, and other breathtaking places in Navajo country. I would also like to thank Carol Perry for her inspiration in helping children on the reservation I am also indebted to Navajo Community College (now Diné College) for many valuable resources used in researching this book. I would also like to acknowledge the assistance of the National Archives, the Library of Congress, the Philbrook Museum, the University of New Mexico Archives, the Amon Carter Museum, and the Northern Arizona University Archives for providing a number of fine illustrations.

I am very much indebted to my editor Kate Nunn for her good humor and hard work in guiding each book in this series from concept to completed manuscript. As always, I would like to thank my wife, Linda, and my children Anna, Sarah, and Luke for their daily inspiration in my life.

MC 12/18/98 91.80L/4V Set

Benchmark Books
Marshall Cavendish Corporation
99 White Plains Road Tarrytown, New York 10591-9001
Text copyright © 1999 by Marshall Cavendish Corporation
Map copyright © 1999 by Marshall Cavendish Corporation
All rights reserved
Library of Congress Cataloging-in-Publication Data
Bial, Raymond. The Navajo / Raymond Bial.
p. cm. — (Lifeways) Includes bibliographical references and index.
Summary: Discusses the history, culture, beliefs, changing ways, and notable people of the Navajo.
ISBN 0-7614-0803-7 1. Navajo Indians—History—Juvenile literature. 3. Navajo Indians—Social life and customs—Juvenile literature. [1. Navajo Indians. 2. Indians of North America—Southwest, New.] I. Title. II. Series: Bial, Raymond. Lifeways.E99.N3B53 1999
973'.04972—DC21 97-53248 CIP AC

Maps by Rodica Prato
Printed in Italy
1 3 5 6 4 2

Cover photos: Raymond Bial

The photographs in this book are used by permission and through the courtesy of:
The Philbrook Museum of Art, Tulsa, OK: 1, 13, 70, 76-77, 79, 81, 86-87. Raymond Bial: 6, 8-9, 20, 22-23, 24, 26-27, 28-29, 36, 37, 39, 40, 43, 44-45, 52-53, 61, 63, 84, 98-99, 100-101, 103, 109, 110-111. Laura Gilpin, courtesy of the Amon Carter Museum: 31, 32, 50, 59, 69, 88-89, 95, 96. Library of Congress: 35, 48, 65. Philip Johnston Collection/Cline Library—NAU: 56. National Archives: 64, 74, 91. UPI/Corbis-Bettmann: 115, 119. R. C. Gorman: 116. Luci Tapahonso: 118.

This book is respectfully dedicated to
all the people who "walk in beauty"
to keep alive the traditional lifeways
of the Navajo.

Contents

1. Origins   8
"The Worlds of Creation" • Land and People

2. A Scattered People   28
Hogans

3. Lifeways   44
Cycle of Life • Gathering and Growing Food •
Recipe: Fry Bread • Clothing • The Gift of Weaving •
"Spider Woman" • Pottery and Baskets • Hunting and
Warfare • Silverwork

4.Beliefs   76
Ceremonies • Drypaintings

5.Changing Ways   88

6.New Ways   100
Navajo Language • Walking in Beauty

More About the Navajo   110
Time Line • Notable People • Glossary • Further
Information

Index   125

Author's Note

At the dawn of the twentieth century, Native Americans were thought to be a vanishing race. However, despite four hundred years of warfare, deprivation, and disease, American Indians have not gone away. Countless thousands have lost their lives, but over the course of this century the populations of native tribes have grown tremendously. Even as American Indians struggle to adapt to modern Western life, they have also kept the flame of their traditions alive—the language, religion, stories, and the everyday ways of life. An exhilarating renaissance in Native American culture is now sweeping the nation from coast to coast.

The *Lifeways* books depict the social and cultural life of the major nations, from the early history of native peoples in North America to their present-day struggles for survival and dignity. Historical and contemporary photographs of traditional subjects, as well as period illustrations, are blended throughout each book so that readers may gain a sense of family life in a tipi, a hogan, or a longhouse.

No single book can comprehensively portray the intricate and varied lifeways of an entire tribe, or nation. I only hope that young people will come away with a deeper appreciation for the rich tapestry of Indian culture—both then and now—and a keen desire to learn more about these first Americans.

1. Origins

The Navajo are deeply attached to their home country. From broad stretches of desert rise majestic stone formations, burnt orange against the setting sun.

THE NAVAJO HAVE NEVER VIEWED HISTORY AS SIMPLY A SERIES OF FACTS about people and events from an earlier time. They conceive of their past and themselves through an intricate weaving of stories about the universe and the supernatural beings who inhabit the world. The Navajo had no written language until recently, so their history has been passed down and interpreted through these tales. To this day, stories guide Navajos along the path to a good life. As Carl Nelson Gorman, a Navajo artist, once said, "Navajo history and mythology are intertwined like strands of a rope."

Geography is also intimately related to Navajo beliefs. Not only do Navajos see their lives as blending with the earth and sky, but every mountain and other distinctive feature of the landscape has its own story, as do the sun, rain, wind, and other elements. Of these stories, the creation, or emergence, lies at the heart of Navajo culture. In this story, insect beings rise through four worlds, each of which is one of the four sacred colors—black, blue, yellow, and white. There are at least sixty versions of this story, and as many as twelve worlds are present in some tellings. Yet each takes us on a spiritual journey in which insects, animals, and people surface through dreamlike worlds until they emerge into the present glittering world of the Navajo people.

"The Worlds of Creation"

In the beginning, there was only the Black World, a small place like a floating island in the center of the dark sea where the holy people lived. They were not people as we know them, but spirits in human form. In the four corners of this world appeared white, blue, yellow, and black columns of clouds, each of which matched one of the four directions. It is said that when Coyote the Trickster visited these clouds he assumed some of their colors, so that he is now the color of the sky at dawn.

The white cloud and black cloud came together in the east, creating the vague figure of First Man and a perfectly shaped ear of white corn. In the west, the yellow cloud and blue cloud met to create First Woman, as well as a perfect ear of yellow corn, a white shell, and a turquoise stone. Standing in the east, First Man burned a crystal, which was the awakening of the mind, and First Woman burned her turquoise. When they saw the light from each other's fire, they came together. First Woman was impressed by the strength of the crystal fire—the clarity of the mind—and when First Man asked her to live with him, she readily agreed.

Different kinds of insect beings—Spider Ants, Wasp People, Ant People, and Beetles—also lived in the Black World. These beings constantly quarreled, and since many knew how to sting with poison, they did great harm to each other. In search of a better place to make their homes, every living creature moved like a cloud, rising through an opening in the east into the Blue World. Here they found many blue-feathered birds—bluebirds, blue jays, and blue hawks. There were also other insect beings, such as crickets and locusts.

As First Man and First Woman journeyed through numerous chambers in the Blue World, they encountered wildcats, wolves, badgers, kit foxes, and mountain lions. These animals warred with each other, and First Man killed some of them. He then brought them back to life when he was given prayers and songs as a reward. Afterward, he wanted to rest, but Coyote and the other beings pleaded to leave the Blue World. So, First Man turned toward the east, and laid down a streak of jagged lightning, straight lightning, rainbow, and finally sun ray. If none of the lightning or rainbow moved, the beings would be able to journey to the next world. He shifted each of these lights to the south, the west, and then the north. There was only the slightest tremble, so he made wands of jet, turquoise, abalone, and white shell on which he placed four footprints. Standing on these footprints, all the beings made a sacrifice and then were carried upward into the Yellow World.

The bluebirds reached the Yellow World first. Next came the First Four (First Man, First Woman, Coyote, and one of the insect beings) and then the others. The Female River flowed across this land north to south, and the Male River went east to west, mingling at a place called Crossing of the Waters. In this world, men and women were meant to live together. There were also six mountains in this land, but no sun. Spider People and many animals, including squirrels, chipmunks, turkeys, lizards, and snakes, lived in the Yellow World. All these creatures, including those that had risen through the previous worlds, still had no clearly defined forms.

Coyote the Trickster slyly asked First Man to give him a piece of white shell. Coyote then took the white shell to a whirlpool and

In this painting by Harrison Begay, Aged Tutor and Young Students, *an elderly man instructs two boys in the complex system of Navajo beliefs.*

found that it could make the water rise and fall like the ocean tides. There he snatched the baby of Water Monster, who became so furious that he caused a great flood to sweep over the land. Gathering earth from each of the six sacred mountains, First Man urged all the beings to flee to White Shell Mountain. The beings hurriedly ascended the mountain, but even at the peak the rising water threatened to overwhelm them. First Man planted a cedar tree and then a pine tree, but neither grew tall enough for them to climb through the ceiling of the sky. He finally planted a female reed, which grew into the heights, and so they climbed to the fourth world—the White, or Glittering, World.

The people noticed that Coyote, who could not be trusted, was hiding the baby of Water Monster. They made him return the child, along with an offering of a white shell basket. This pacified Water Monster, who ended the flood. In the Glittering World, First Man and First Woman created the four sacred mountains from the earth that First Man had collected in the Yellow World. They also placed the stars, the sun, and the moon in the sky. After they made day and night and the four seasons, they planted the perfect seed corn they had brought with them and harvested the first crops. They learned to create fire, build houses, called hogans, and sweat lodges. They played the moccasin game to amuse themselves but also became sadly acquainted with death. To their dismay, they discovered that terrible monsters inhabited the Glittering World.

At dawn, First Man and First Woman came upon a baby girl crying from within a cloud hovering over Gobernador Knob near

Huerfano Mountain. The couple decided to take care of the baby, who was born of mingled dawn and night. They named her Changing Woman, and she became one of the most beloved beings of the Navajo people. When she was on the verge of becoming an adult, Changing Woman took part in a ceremony called *Kinaaldá*, which enabled her to always "walk in beauty." Sometime later, she wandered away from her hogan and fell asleep near a waterfall. There, she was visited by the Sun who sent a ray of his light through the mist of the cascading water and impregnated her. She gave birth to twin sons, whom she named Monster Slayer and Born for Water, both of whom were destined to become strong warriors and skillful hunters.

Because of the monsters, the Glittering World was not safe, so the two boys had to be careful when they wandered from their hogan. While hunting one day they came upon a hole in the ground from which a voice beckoned, "Come in." The hole widened, and the twins descended a ladder, where they met Spider Woman. They asked if she knew who their father was, so they could ask him how to kill the monsters. "Your father is the Sun," she told them. Spider Woman then agreed to help the boys on their dangerous journey to find their father and ask him for help. She gave them an eagle feather, a white shell, and turquoise to make their hearts strong. She warned them of the fierce guardians and told them the prayers they must utter on the way to the Sun's house.

The twins had to travel over sharp reeds that could have

shredded them. They crossed drifting sands that could have smothered them. They crept through canyons whose walls could have crushed them. They had to cross a flooded stream on the back of a worm and the ocean on the back of a water skeeter.

The twins finally arrived at the Sun's house, which was guarded by the Great Snake, the Black Bear, the Big Thunder, and the Big Wind. But chanting prayers from Spider Woman, they safely passed the guards and entered the house. The Sun refused to admit that he was their father until the twins underwent a series of tests. The Sun flung them in turn against white spikes on the eastern wall of his house, turquoise spikes on the southern wall, yellow spikes on the western wall, and black spikes on the northern wall, but the brothers were not injured. He then asked them to smoke a deadly tobacco, but they were not harmed. He also subjected them to a hot sweat bath and fed them poisoned cornmeal, but they survived all these ordeals.

After the twins had passed these challenges, the Sun gave "Lightning That Strikes Crooked" to Monster Slayer and "Lightning That Flashes Straight" to Born for Water, along with suits of flint armor. He also presented them with gifts of the sun—rainbow, lightning, and mirage—as well as mist and rain. With these powerful weapons, the twins killed all the monsters, except those that cause hunger, old age, and death. Because of the knowledge of Spider Woman and the courage of Changing Woman's sons, the Glittering World at last became safe for the Navajo people, who to this day live in its sacred land.

LIKE OTHER INDIANS, THE ANCESTORS OF THE NAVAJO (pronounced NAH-vah-hoe) originally came from Siberia, probably crossing a narrow land bridge into what is now Alaska. For thousands of years they lived in what is today Alaska and the Canadian Northwest, speaking an Athapaskan language, as did the other tribes living there. Hundreds of years ago, between A.D. 1000 and 1500, the people who became the Navajo migrated into the highlands of the American Southwest. Like their cousins the Apaches, the Navajos are linked by language to these northern peoples. They also tell some of the same stories to this very day.

The Navajo past remains filled with mysteries. Why, after thousands of years in the frozen north, did they discard their snowshoes and migrate all the way to the arid lands of present-day New Mexico and Arizona? Are Navajo hogans based on wickiups, the small huts made by Northwest Indians of supple willow branches covered with animal skins? Why did these people, who originally lived by the Pacific Ocean, once have a taboo against eating fish? Why are the Navajo, along with the Apache, the only Athapaskan-speaking people to be found between the northern coast and the southern deserts?

It is believed that most of the Navajos came in a large, single burst of migration to the parched land around Gobernado Canyon. Navajo creation stories place their emergence here. Small groups, or bands, of hunters—men, women, and children dressed in animal skins—followed over the next several generations. Later, as their way of life changed, the people drifted into two distinct

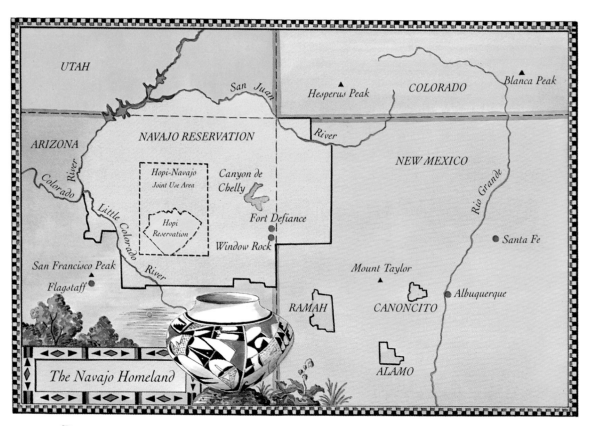

Utah
Arizona
San Juan
Navajo Reservation
Hopi-Navajo Joint Use Area
Canyon de Chelly
Colorado River
Little Colorado River
Hopi Reservation
Fort Defiance
Window Rock
San Francisco Peak
Flagstaff
The Navajo Homeland
Ramah
Hesperus Peak
Colorado
Blanca Peak
River
New Mexico
Rio Grande
Santa Fe
Mount Taylor
Canoncito
Albuquerque
Alamo

*T*raditional Navajo lands extended over most of what is now northeastern Arizona as well as present-day Utah and New Mexico.

groups: the wandering Apache and the more settled Navajo, a name given to them by the Spanish. The Spanish *Navajó* is derived from the Tewa Indian word *Navahu'*, meaning "large planted fields." *Apachu* is most likely derived from the Zuni word for "enemy." Originally called Apaches de Navahú, the Navajo refer to themselves as Diné (din-NAY), which in their language means "person." The first European encounters with Navajo and Apache people occurred in the Black Mesa country of present-day northern Arizona and were recorded by Spanish missionaries in 1626 and 1630.

Hardy and clever, the Navajo made weapons and tools from wood and stone. While the men hunted, the women and children gathered berries, nuts, and bulbs. The Navajo were also highly adaptable—in fact, their ability to learn from other people became a distinctive feature of their culture. From the time the Navajo arrived in the Southwest, Pueblo culture exerted a strong influence on their way of life. Fierce raiders, as well as warriors, the Navajo plundered the storehouses of the neighboring Pueblo Indians, who grew corn, beans, and squash. They also kidnapped Pueblo women, who became wives and mothers and taught the Navajo new and useful skills, such as the cultivation of crops.

Highly inventive themselves, the Navajo used a sinew-backed bow that was very powerful and accurate. They also fashioned a moccasin boot that protected their calves from the cactus and thorny bushes of the desert country. Yet, after their migration, their society was markedly shaped by their interaction with the Pueblos.

The Navajo learned about farming and other life skills from the Pueblo Indians, who lived in villages. Many of these settlements were built into cliffs, which protected the inhabitants from enemies.

When they encountered the Spanish in the 1600s, they had already largely abandoned a nomadic way of life and were cultivating fields, weaving baskets, and making clay pots. From the Spanish, they quickly learned the value of horses, sheep, and cattle. Until that time, like many other American Indians, their only domesticated animal was the dog. By trading and raiding, however, they became expert horsemen and began to raise flocks of sheep and goats. From sheep came both meat and fluffy wool, which the Navajo wove into lovely blankets and rugs. Over the generations, weaving became an inherent part of the Navajo way of life.

Land and People

I see the Earth.
I am looking at her and smile
Because she makes me happy.
The Earth, looking back at me
Is smiling too.
May I walk happily
And lightly
Upon her.

—Navajo song

For hundreds of years, the Navajo have lived in the *Dinetah*, a vast, fabled homeland that extends over much of northeastern Arizona and western New Mexico, as well as parts of Utah and Colorado—about fifteen million acres with few people. It is also a country of many elevations. The land rises from deep canyons, in which ancient ruins are tucked away on the rock ledges, to towering mountain ranges streaked with pink, black, and white layers of rock.

At lower elevations, the Canyon de Chelly (shay), which once sheltered cliff dwellers, cuts jaggedly through the landscape. The desert floor, with its sands in shades of brown from light tan to deep chocolate, is punctuated by tabletop mesas and the striking wind-sculpted sandstone formations of Monument Valley. Shimmering with mirages, there is also the brilliance of the Painted

Navajo country is marked by deep canyons as well as towering mountains. Here, in the fertile bottomland of Canyon de Chelly, farmers plant fields of corn and other crops.

Desert. The landscape changes from pale green sage, greasewood, yucca, and brittle grass undulating in the winds to the higher plateaus dotted with deep emerald piñon, juniper, and rabbit bush. The terrain continues to rise steadily until it's overtaken by forests of pine and fir trees in the mountains. In every direction, there are sweeping panoramas and puffy white clouds sailing through the crisp blue sky.

The traditional Navajo homeland is marked in each direction by the four sacred mountains: *Sis Naajini* (Blanca Peak) in the east; *Doo Ko' oosliid* (San Francisco Peaks) in the west; *Tso dzilh* (Mount Taylor) in the south; and *Di-be Nitsaa'* (Hesperus Peak) in the north. Although the Navajo may not physically be able to see all four peaks from their hogans, in their hearts they know that from these sacred places come the plants, animals, and minerals for

*E*verything in nature is sacred to the Navajo, not only plants and animals but also rocks and soil. Jutting upward, this rock formation catches the last rays of light at the end of the day.

their religious ceremonies. This knowledge provides comfort and strength to the Navajo people, whether they live on the reservation or far away.

Many wild animals have adapted to this rugged country: long-legged jackrabbits with large, scooping ears; coiled rattlesnakes with ominously vibrating tails; and scrawny peccaries, snorting and squealing as they scuttle through the brush. And there is the crafty coyote, always keeping its distance, always up to no good, as it trots along at the edge of the horizon, that thin line between land and sky. Mountain lions and bears make their home here, too, as does the sacred horned toad, which is considered the grandfather of all the Navajo.

To the Navajos, everything is alive, not just these animals and the beloved plants, but the sun, rain, air, and earth. And the wind, which swirls over the land and comes out of one's mouth as breath, gives life to one and all. In the skin whorls at the tips of their fingers, people can see the trail of the winds. Each creature and element has a story, often told by the Navajo, who deeply love the land throughout the days and seasons of their lives. The parched earth receives little rain, and the water that does fall usually comes in a powerful storm that floods sandy creek beds called washes. As the saying goes, the rivers are "a mile wide and an inch deep." The land then bursts with foliage and flowers above the rose, purple, and chocolate of soil and rocks. However, most often, from first light to dusk, the sun pulses brightly overhead. The huge blue bowl of sky threatens to overwhelm those who live beneath it, except that through the crystal clear air one can see miles upon miles of gorgeous land.

Scattered among the sage and rocks are small hogans and other shelters—a shade, a brush circle, or perhaps a sheep corral. The next hogan or other sign of human life may be miles down the road—tucked beside a cliff or nestled among the pines. Small herds of cattle may graze in the distance or horses may make their way up a hillside, but the dry land is most suitable for grazing sheep. Old women in long skirts with kerchiefs tied over their

Fabled Monument Valley reaches into the southern part of present-day Utah. This rugged, sacred land is noted for its striking buttes, which rise up from the dry red sand and sparse foliage.

heads watch over the shaggy flocks with the help of quick, bright-eyed dogs.

The Navajo hold this land as sacred—it is their Glittering World. Whether it is the Three Sisters of Monument Valley, or Window Rock, or Rainbow Bridge, the land is the source of both food to sustain the body and knowledge to enliven the soul. This wondrous land is best described in the words of a Navajo prayer: "Beauty before me, beauty behind me, beauty above me, beauty beneath me."

2. A Scattered People

The shape of the conical hogan is based on the description in the creation story of the hogan built by First Man. The wood frame was covered with mud, which made the dwelling cool in summer and warm in winter.

UNLIKE THE APACHES, THE NAVAJOS GRADUALLY ABANDONED THEIR nomadic ways as hunters and gatherers, and settled down to a life as farmers and herders. Unlike other Athapaskan peoples, they also adopted a society of matrilineal clans from the western Pueblos. The clans included several extended families who considered themselves related—not only mothers and fathers, children, and grandparents, but also aunts and uncles (sisters and brothers of the mother). Sons and daughters were not allowed to marry within their own or their father's clan. Women headed households within the clan and children traced their heritage through their mother's side of the family. Originally, there were just four clans—today there are over sixty clans in the Navajo Nation. In these clans, all property is also handed down through the mother's side of the family.

At the time of Spanish contact the Navajo were scarcely a unified people, let alone a single nation. Unlike the Pueblo, who lived in villages, the Navajo scattered themselves over the vast stretches of desert, plateaus, and high country between the four sacred mountains. Allegiances were narrowly defined to include only those living nearby—family, clan, and immediate neighbors. A community simply formed around a group of hogans at a crossing of two trails in the desert. The Navajos did not have one leader or a central government. Rather, small, independent bands, usually a clan or groups of clans, were led by a *naat'aani*, or headman, who had excellent speaking skills and a thorough knowledge of Navajo ceremonies. Other men provided leadership

During the heat of summer, the family often lived in a shade, or ramada. The tree branches deflected the hot sun but allowed the cool evening breezes to drift through the home.

During a long drought in Navajo country, water is terribly scarce. This young man had to drive his herd of sheep eight miles over rough terrain to reach this pool of water in the shelter of the rocks.

in hunting, warfare, and curing ceremonies. *Hózhoojí naat'ááh* served as peace leaders in these loosely organized bands.

The arrival of the Spanish further changed Navajo culture and social life. Although missionaries had very few converts, the Spanish brought horses, sheep, and cattle. Navajo men eagerly traded for the animals, but more often they raided the Spanish herds. By caring for domesticated sheep, they no longer had to rely entirely on wild game as a source of meat in their diet. They so thoroughly made sheep and horses part of their everyday life that it is now difficult to imagine the Navajo without them. Even the Navajo consider themselves ancient herders, as indicated by one man's observation: "Since time immemorial our grandfathers and our grandmothers have lived from their herds—from their herds of sheep, horses, and cattle, for those things originated with the world itself."

In the span of just three centuries, from the late 1400s to the early 1700s, the Navajo acquired a new culture built upon the myth of emergence, and adapted to very different ways of providing for themselves. They learned many new skills from the Pueblos and the Spanish without abandoning their own language and traditional culture.

Hogans

One feature of Navajo life that has endured to the present is the hogan (from the word *hooghan* meaning "home"). Whatever their location or style, hogans are revered as homes and places of worship, their design ordained by the gods. Just as the dome of the sky was viewed as a hogan, so the hogan itself symbolized the universe. In Navajo belief, the original hogan was built by First Man and First Woman, its poles made of jewels: white shell, abalone, turquoise, and jet. When finished, this hogan was too small to hold all of the beings on Earth, so it was expanded by blowing on the poles. The hogan was then praised in song, along with its contents and the rainbow that arced overhead. Consecrated in a special Blessingway Ceremony, the hogan became a sacred place. Corn pollen, a symbol of fertility, was sprinkled on the hogan as the medicine man, or chanter, offered a prayer for a long and happy life for the inhabitants.

One family usually lived in each hogan, but its members might include not only children and their parents, but also grandparents and aunts and uncles, as well as distant blood relatives. Hogans were most often situated far from anyone else's home—the farther the better. Whether domed, cone-shaped, or multi-sided, these dwellings had no windows or furniture—only sheepskin bedding, a few pots, clothes, and other belongings. The single door always faced east, toward the rising sun, to greet each new day. Water, which was precious in the desert, was usually hauled from the nearest creek or spring. People often had to travel great distances to gather firewood.

Early Navajo lived in dugouts with no doors—just a yucca or grass mat roof. People climbed in and out through the smoke hole by means of a ladder. Later, they built homes by piling stones along cliff walls and laying poles overhead for a roof. Sometimes, they occupied abandoned cliff dwellings. For hundreds of years, however, they lived in many different kinds of hogans—and many people still do. Hogan styles have varied over time and by region, but may be grouped into four types: forked-stick, or male hogans (rarely found today); hogans made of upright posts topped with horizontal logs and covered with mud; hogans with horizontal logs laid in a hexagonal or octagonal pattern; and beehive-style hogans.

Forked-stick hogans were made of deadwood, usually pine, because the early Navajo respected all living plants and, in any case, did not have axes to chop down trees. They also liked pine because of its straight grain, although this wood decayed more quickly than juniper and piñon. (Spruce, which was considered a

One or more families often lived together in a single circular room. This hogan, with its doorway facing east, was located in the valley of Canyon de Chelly.

sacred wood, was never used in making hogans.) Builders leaned three posts together so the ends forked at the peak, creating a three-dimensional triangle. The south pole interlocked with the north pole, and both were held in the fork of the west pole. They next laid smaller poles between them and either plastered these cone-shaped structures with mud or left the poles bare.

Similar to the forked-stick hogan, the four-legged hogan consisted of four upright posts and crossbeams around which other poles were laid at a slight angle. When mud or clay was

This forked-stick hogan was built in the middle of the vast dry country. Not a single other home was located within sight, and one could see for miles in every direction.

*T*o make the conical roof of the hogan, rows of logs were laid closer together. A hole in the center allowed the smoke from the fire to escape.

applied to the outside, this hogan looked like an earthen mound. Builders always left a smoke hole slightly off-center. Mats woven from yucca or grass, as well as juniper bark, were hung over the doorway to keep out the wind and cold.

In recent times, the Navajo constructed beehive hogans, with six or eight sides, in which logs were laid vertically, slightly closer together from the bottom to the top of the roof, and plastered with mud to resemble an igloo. Sometimes, they brought the walls up vertically, laying the logs closer together at the top to make a domed roof. They threw soil on this roof to deflect the hot sun and shed the occasional rain. These beehive hogans are often seen on the Navajo reservation today, along with those made of milled lumber and plywood sheathing.

While building a hogan, the men kept a fire burning on the dirt floor in the center of the rising walls—ceremonies and other important events that honored the cycle of life always took place in the presence of fire. Considered every Navajo's mother, the fire provided warmth and light, as well as heat for cooking foods. The hogan, when finished, was dedicated in a ceremony called the Blessingway to insure good fortune for those who lived within its walls. Sprinkling an offering of cornmeal on the walls, the creators of the hogan offered thanks to the white beads, turquoise, abalone, and jet—the materials from which it was believed the first hogan was made. Stone slabs, which outlasted wood, were sometimes set in the ground near the doorway in hopes of a long life for the hogan and its song.

Navajo families usually came together to live in their hogans during the winter months. Because firewood was scarce it made sense for people to share the warmth of one hogan instead of many different homes. With many people living inside the hogan, the Navajo had to treat each other with respect. They followed old customs that gave each person and object its proper place. Women always sat on the north side and men on the south. Children stayed near their mothers, and the place of honor for the elders was the west side facing the doorway. Goods were either stacked against the walls or hung from the roof logs. Cooking utensils were kept near the fire or stove. Along the west side were the sheepskin

In more recent years, the Navajo made hogan walls of logs laid lengthwise.
The roof logs were laid increasingly closer together and covered with mud,
which gave them a rounded shape that readily shed rain.

bedrolls used for visiting during the day, storytelling in the evening, and sleeping at night. Clothes were also usually stored in this area, and blankets—worn over the shoulder in warm weather or wrapped around the shoulders during the winter—were hung on horizontal poles.

It was believed that ceremonial knowledge resided in the north,

To build a ramada, large tree limbs are laid across four upright corner posts. Additional smaller branches fill in the sides and the roof.

so people hung ritual herbs from the roof logs and stored sacred minerals, as well as ceremonial belongings, in this part of the hogan. Tools to battle the evils of hunger and poverty, such as the man's hunting and silverworking equipment and the woman's grinding stones, were also kept here. Jewelry, like sheep, was quite valuable; it could be pawned, traded, or sold to keep away hunger, so it was hung on the north wall, although often concealed beneath clothing. Gambling and games of chance also took place on the north side of the hogan. These were considered powerful forms of knowledge. By gambling, one learned about taking risks, making the right decisions, and knowing when to cease an activity. Gambling embodied not only skill, but the discipline through which one learned responsible behavior.

Near the hogan, families built "shades" called *ramadas*, which resembled open porches. They constructed these shades with upright piñon corner posts and crossbeams. Laying more poles on the top and sides, they covered the frame with juniper branches, leaving an open doorway facing the rising sun. Traditionally, the hogan was the winter home. During the hot summer, the shade became a more comfortable home. People sometimes cooked and slept there, cooled by the evening breezes. Often, women set up their looms and, sheltered from the baking heat of the sun, wove blankets and rugs in the shade. Corn was often dried on the roof because of the good air circulation.

The Navajo also built sweat lodges, or steam baths, near their hogans. Most often, these small hogans were dug into the side of a hill, with the doorway also facing east. Men brought hot stones into the lodges over which they sprinkled water to fill the interior with refreshing steam. The hot steam not only opened the pores of the skin but purified the spirit. While in the sweat lodge, the men chanted songs and invited the holy people to join them. Invisible spiritual beings, the holy people taught the Navajo to be strengthened by the earth and to conduct themselves properly in everyday life.

When hunting or setting up a sheep camp, people often built a windbreak called a brush circle. These shelters were made by simply arranging dried branches in a circle. Sometimes, newly married couples lived in a nearby brush circle while the head mother stayed in the hogan, or the newlyweds built a hogan near the home of the bride's mother. Over time, as daughters married, other hogans came to be clustered around the mother's home, like chicks around a hen. To keep peace among families, one of the oldest Navajo beliefs was that a husband and mother-in-law must not speak directly to each other. If they had anything to say to each other, they had to communicate through a third person.

Hogans usually had a sheep corral nearby. Because of sparse grazing, sheep were herded over large expanses of desert, but at night they were kept in pens made of tree branches. Among their hardy breeds of sheep, most Navajo kept several Angora goats with large, twisted horns, whose fine mohair was—and still is—highly prized by rug weavers.

Occasionally people made their home in brush circles like this one, at least until they were able to build a hogan of their own. Sometimes they held religious ceremonies within the thin walls of swirling branches.

3. Lifeways

This loom was set up in the dappled shade of a ramada. For generations, Navajo women have used such looms to weave wool fibers into durable and lovely rugs and blankets.

OVER THE CENTURIES, NAVAJO LIFE CHANGED DRAMATICALLY. YET both young and old people remained deeply attached to their families and the land. The mother and the place of one's birth were especially honored. In the home, the baby in his cradleboard was placed so he could gaze into his mother's face, as well as about the world—from the warm glow of the fire within the hogan to the mountains rising in the distance. Here, each child grew up encircled by the clan. Here, every boy and girl learned the enduring ways of the Navajo. Here, young women and young men, coming of age, joined in marriage and brought the next generation of children into the world.

Cycle of Life

Birth. From the moment of birth, the Navajo followed sacred rituals. Long after the introduction of iron into their culture, they still used a flint blade to cut the baby's umbilical cord, which was then buried in the ground near the birthplace.

The woman who had assisted the delivery had the honor of bathing the newborn. The baby was then placed at the mother's left side, his head toward the north and the fire, and anointed with corn pollen, a sacred symbol of life among the Navajo.

The father made a cradleboard for the baby that had three parts: frame, back slats, and hoop. The hoop protected the baby's head in case the cradleboard toppled over and shaded the baby's eyes from the glare of the sun. As the baby was swaddled in layers of cloth and strapped to the cradleboard, the Navajo chanted a song :

> *I have made a baby board for you*
> *my son [or daughter]*
> *May you grow to a great old age*
> *Of the sun's rays I have made the back*
> *Of black clouds I have made the blanket*
> *Of rainbow I have made the bow*
> *Of sunbeams I have made the side loops*
> *Of sun dogs I have made the footboard*
> *Of dawn I have made the covering*
> *Of black fog I have made the bed.*

Much of the baby's first year was spent in the cradleboard. Well adapted to the Navajo way of life, the cradleboard could be strapped to the mother's back, or stood upright against the side of the hogan or a tree so the baby could see its mother while she was weaving at the loom or preparing meals. While nestled in the cradleboard, the baby was also less likely to be bothered by snakes and insects. When the mother traveled on horseback, she simply tied the cradleboard to the saddle horn and trotted across the sage.

At six or seven months of age, the baby began to spend some time out of the cradleboard, learning to crawl and being held by its mother and other relatives. Because mothers were often busy, older girls in the family helped look after the baby.

This young mother carries her baby in a cradleboard strapped to her back. Her hands are free—to cultivate corn, gather firewood, cook a meal, or weave a rug—while the baby gazes out upon the world.

Coming-of-Age. Good and loving parents, the Navajo seldom punished their children. Yet children were scarcely spoiled. Having few toys, they became quite resourceful in inventing their own games. As soon as they were old enough, they were also expected to help around the hogan, carrying firewood or tending the sheep.

Growing up among many relatives, children not only learned the practical skills of providing for themselves, they also received instruction in the customs of their people. They learned about the holy people and the many intricate rituals associated with their beliefs.

When boys and girls came of age, a special ceremony called *Yeibichai* was held. Toward the end of the ceremony, two men wearing scary masks jumped out at the children. After the dance, they removed the masks, and the children discovered they were relatives. The children then put on the masks and peered through the eyeholes, so they would be relieved of their fears and feel grown-up.

When they reached puberty, girls were honored in a *Kinaaldá* ceremony so that, like Changing Woman, they might always "walk in beauty."

Marriage. Marriage, which brought the promise of more children, was considered the most important social responsibility. Traditionally, a young man who wished to court a young woman appeared at her home with a deer slung over his shoulder as a gift for her family. He thus showed the parents that he was a

This father, a modern medicine man, poses proudly with his three children among the pines high up in the mountains.

good provider. In recent years, he more likely brought a sleek horse as a gift. If his proposal was accepted, the wedding was planned.

During the marriage, the bride and her family sat along the west and south, or the female, side of the hogan; the groom and his family sat along the east and north, or male side. The bride and groom ritually washed each other's hands. The medicine man then blessed the couple and the cornmeal mush in the wedding basket by sprinkling corn pollen in two lines to unite the male and female knowledge that resides in the four sacred mountains. Beginning in the east, the medicine man next sprinkled cornmeal in a circle; the newlyweds and their guests ate some cornmeal mush from each of the four sides of the basket, beginning with the east, honoring the path of the sun and each of the sacred directions.

The groom often moved into the hogan of his bride's mother or grandmother, or the couple might settle into a smaller hogan nearby. The newlyweds' hogan was anointed with corn pollen in hopes of bringing future happiness. Throughout their marriage the couple sought the help of the holy people to "keep their feet in the Blessingway."

Death. The Navajo viewed death, especially a violent, unnatural death, as a break in the cycle of life. It was a dangerous, uncertain time—ghosts of dead people often turned evil and brought harm to the living. If the death took place inside the hogan, the body could not be carried out the door. A hole was knocked through the north side of the hogan, and the deceased was carried out the

The river winding through the deep gorge of Canyon de Chelly is an oasis Navajo farmers have relied on for centuries.

back. The hogan, with everything inside, was then abandoned.

The body had to be buried immediately to return the deceased to the four elements from which everything was created: earth, air, fire, and water. It was believed that the natural cycle of life began when these elements first came together in the womb of a woman.

Gathering and Growing Food

When the Navajo moved to the Southwest hundreds of years ago, girls and women gathered wild plants, seeds, and berries to help feed their families and to provide herbal medicines. Every spring, summer, and fall, they journeyed to different regions—

desert, grasslands, or mountains. Men usually did not help in collecting but often accompanied the women to protect them from animals and enemies.

Of the many foods provided by plants, the most important were mescal (also known as agave) and piñon nuts. The spiked heads of the mescal plant were taken apart, baked in rock-lined underground ovens, dried in the sun, and put away for the winter. The dried mescal was sometimes pounded into sheets, which could be stored for a longer time. In the autumn, girls and women traveled to the forests and gathered piñon nuts. They either collected the pine cones from the forest floor or shook them out of the trees. The nuts were roasted, shelled, and ground into piñon flour, which was used to make tasty bread. Piñon flour was also put into soups. Some nuts were left in their shells to be eaten whole later.

Because of the dry, clear weather, many foods were sun-dried and stored in baskets or other containers. People left some of these foodstuffs in hiding places and took the rest with them. These hiding places were known as caches. They could simply be a hole dug into the side of a hill, but the Navajo preferred caves, which remained high and dry. After placing the food inside, they sealed the opening with rocks and dirt. Throughout the year, they returned to the caches as they needed more food.

Over time, the adaptable Navajo learned to grow corn from the Pueblos who lived near them, and partly abandoned their nomadic way of life. Setting up summer camps, girls and women planted their seeds. The oldest and youngest members of the band then stayed to tend the cornfields while the others journeyed to hunt and gather other foods. Corn became the most important crop, but people also began to plant beans and squash. When the Spanish arrived, they brought other new crops, including potatoes, peaches, and wheat, and the Navajo became accomplished farmers.

Corn was sometimes eaten fresh, as corn on the cob, or dried in ovens and then stored. Women dried corn in a type of stone and adobe oven used by the Spanish. After burning a fire in the beehive-shaped oven all day, they raked out the coals. Placing the ears of corn and a little water inside, they closed the door and let the corn dry all night. In the morning, they scraped the kernels from the cobs and spread them in the sun to complete the drying process. Dried corn could be used immediately or stored for months. Women usually ground the kernels between two stones to make cornmeal, which was used in tortillas, tamales, soups, mushes, and corn cakes.

Women often baked and boiled corn and other foods over an open fire in the center of the hogan, the smoke rising through the hole in the roof. During warm months, they cooked out in the yard or in the ramada. When the Navajo began to herd sheep, they also began to eat more lamb and mutton and came to rely less on wild game. Today, women may cook on a small woodstove, instead of an open fire, but they have prepared the same or similar meals, spiced with hot Mexican chilies, for over two hundred years now.

While her children look on, this Navajo woman methodically pushes a curved stone against another larger stone to grind dried corn kernels. The coarse yellow meal will be used to make bread and other traditional dishes.

Here's a modern version of a popular traditional dish, which substitutes white flour for cornmeal.

Fry Bread

Ingredients:

4 cups white flour
1 tablespoon baking powder
1 teaspoon salt
1½ cups water
Cooking oil

Mix the dry ingredients in a large bowl. When they are thoroughly mixed, add the 1½ cups water and knead until the dough is soft and does not stick to the bowl. If necessary, add a little more water.

Form the dough into balls about the size of plums. Pat the dough back and forth in your hands to flatten the balls until they become round pancake-like patties about ¼ to ½ inch thick. Heat ½ inch cooking oil in a heavy frying pan. Carefully place the patties in the frying pan and brown on both sides. Drain the fry bread on paper towels and serve hot.

Another type of bread made by the Navajo is kneel-down bread, made of sweet corn kernels wrapped in cornhusks and baked in hot coals. Loaves of blue corn bread are made with juniper ashes and blue cornmeal. Paper bread is made of the same ingredients flattened and then fried. The Navajo also made other interesting dishes, such as blue cake, corn and cheese pudding, and meat jerky, as well as lamb stew and lamb loaf.

Clothing

In addition to gathering berries, raising corn, and preparing meals, women made all the clothing for their families. Traditionally, they used the hides of deer and other wild animals—rabbits, bears, coyotes, fox, badger, wildcats, and mountain lions—as well as pronghorn antelope, mountain goats, and mountain sheep to make leather clothing and moccasins. Men stretched the hides over a post leaning against a tree, then scraped away the fat and meat with sharpened horse ribs or flint blades. Later, they switched to metal tools. To make rawhide, women took fresh or dried skins—most often deerskins—rubbed them with fat and buried them in the damp soil for a day or so. The skins were then spread over a large rock and beaten with a stone. After scraping the hair from the skins, they greased them with fat again, this time near a fire. They buried the skins in wet earth once more, for about three days, after which they were considered dressed. Women used the tough, stiff rawhide to make moccasin soles and robes, as well as thongs and cords. They also tanned deerskins

This Navajo girl is wearing a dress and jewelry typical of the 1880s. The old-style attire of both men and women was heavily influenced by the neighboring Pueblo Indians and Spanish settlers.

and other animal hides to make supple buckskin. First they washed the hides in cold water and then twisted and pulled them to make them soft. They next soaked the hides in a liquid made by boiling the animal's brain in water. After hanging the hides to dry, they soaked them once more in water and stretched them until they became soft and pliable.

After the arrival of the Spanish, the Navajo adopted new clothing materials and styles. Girls and women began to wear handwoven mantas, or shawls, over their long, buckskin dresses. Over time, they abandoned buckskin in favor of a Spanish style of cloth dresses, loose blouses, and long skirts. Boys and men also dressed like their Mexican and Pueblo neighbors in shirts and white pants that ended halfway between the knee and ankle. They also often wore headbands of twisted cloth or a strip of fur. Both men and women decorated the seams of their clothing with silver buttons. Men began to drape blankets over their shoulders like Mexicans, and women wore them as large fringed shawls.

In the 1860s, when the United States imprisoned the Navajo at a place called Bosque Redondo, women began to wear full, ankle-length skirts given to them by the American soldiers' wives. They later traded for calico and made their own skirts. Men wore coats and pants supplied to them by the Indian Agency after the Treaty of 1868. As time went by, the Navajo continued to adopt new clothing styles. Women came to prefer velveteen blouses in a variety of bright colors, which they decorated with silver buttons made from flattened Mexican pesos. Their apparel was

Girls and women wear long, loose-fitting skirts and blouses. If they can afford to do so, they also adorn themselves with silver and turquoise jewelry.

complemented with leather belts adorned with strings of silver conchas, or shells. Both men and women wore strings of turquoise, shell, coral, or silver beads. Men came to wear silk scarves as headbands, or they sported wide-brimmed black hats.

Today, the Navajo blend elements of clothing styles from the past and the present—Indian, Spanish, and Anglo. Women wear jeans and T-shirts, but also colorful blouses and full satin skirts. Men also like jeans and cowboy boots and often wear their hair in a long braid. Both men and women continue to adorn themselves with beautifully crafted silver and turquoise jewelry.

The Gift of Weaving

When the Spanish introduced livestock—horses, cattle, sheep, goats, and pigs to the Southwest—the Navajo soon found sheep and goats to be invaluable as a source of food, clothing, and trade goods. The raising of sheep, the spinning of wool, and the weaving of textiles have since become a distinctive Navajo art form. Women wove the sheep's wool and the goats' mohair into blankets for their own use. They also exchanged rugs and blankets at the trading posts that came to be established in their home country. Sheep also replaced deer as the primary source of meat in their diet. As the Navajo concentrated on their flocks and fields, they became even less like their Apache cousins who continued to live as hunters and gatherers. To this day, the Navajo judge themselves by the size and quality of their flocks of sheep. Descended from a breed brought by the Spanish, the sheep are small, tough animals, able to withstand the desert heat, cold winters, and sudden changes in weather, as well as subsist on meager amounts of food and water.

After the sheep were sheared, women washed the wool (if it was oily) with pounded yucca roots, which made a nice, sudsy water. The wool was then carded, or combed, with two spiked boards to remove burrs, pebbles, and other debris, and to align the fibers. The wool was finally spun, or twisted, using a round spindle to make a long, continuous thread. The colors of the wool thread included the natural white, black, gray, and brown of the sheep. Sometimes they also made dyes—green from sagebrush, violet from holly berries, yellow from goldenrod, orange from lichens, brown from piñon trees, and red from mahogany roots. Deep blue came from the indigo, another natural dye, but one that was purchased from travelers. For bright red, Navajo women raveled bayenta, an imported woolen cloth, and re-used the yarn.

Seated in the yard outside the hogan, they wove rugs, blankets, and serapes, their fingers nimbly working the yarn across the warp of the loom, building the designs. The terms "blanket" and "rug" are misleading because Navajo textiles have never been intended primarily as bedding or floor covers. Actually, they are multi-purpose items for wearing, sleeping, bartering, and gift giving. A woman worked about two hundred hours to make a three-by-five-

This woman spent many weeks weaving this small rug. The turquoise color comes from modern dye, while the white threads and rich shades of brown are the natural colors of the wool from her sheep and goats.

*W*ith her loom and a portion of clear sky in the background, this woman spins wool into thread. Instead of a spinning wheel, Navajo women use a spool, which they roll with their fingers to make thread from tufts of wool.

foot blanket. Since she had cooking, washing, and other chores, it usually took her several months to complete a single blanket.

During the summer, women usually did their weaving in a brush shade, while in the winter they set up their wood-frame looms on the south side of the hogan. They offered prayers and songs of thanks for the sheep that supplied the wool, for the plants from which they made the dyes, and for the trees that provided wood for the loom and weaving tools. Women wove with a sense of their place within time and the universe. For example, since vertical warps represented rain, it was not proper to weave during a rainstorm. This was considered a sign of greed—wishing for rain when it was already raining.

Originally, the Navajo made striped blankets modeled after Pueblo designs, but they soon created their own strikingly original patterns. Major weaves included wedge weave (which is uniquely Navajo), herringbone (for saddle blankets), two-faced blankets (with a different pattern on each side), and diamond twill (there are several kinds of twills). Over time the design of blankets included matching bands separated by a central band or decoration. Zigzag patterns represented male lightning, while straight lines symbolized female lightning. Terraced patterns imitated clouds, and parallelograms stood for desert mist. By

Navajo women weave a large rug at a loom set up outside. Strapped in a cradleboard at the foot of the loom, a baby looks on while sheep wander nearby.

weaving these designs into their blankets, Navajo women honored and gave thanks for the natural elements around them.

Typically, young women wore blankets of brighter colors and more active designs, including male lightning, to attract a husband. Older women preferred more subdued colors depicting clouds or female rain. Young children often wore blankets with mountains-of-knowledge designs against a field of white in hopes of a happy future.

Today, the Navajo prefer soft, brightly colored Pendleton blankets with Navajo designs because they are less expensive than handwoven blankets. During ceremonies, women and men always wear blankets, whatever the season and weather. The blanket represents the cornhusk, and the wearer's flowing, unbraided hair symbolizes the corn silk. Thus, the individual becomes a metaphor for corn, a primary source of life for the Navajo. To this day, women credit Spider Woman for the gift of weaving.

"Spider Woman"

At the time of creation, when the people emerged from the third world and entered the fourth, they encountered Spider Woman. Monsters roamed the land and killed many people, but Spider Woman loved the people and gave power to Monster Slayer and Born for Water to search for their father the Sun. When the twins found their father, he showed them how they could destroy all the monsters on the land and in the water.

Because Spider Woman had helped to save them, the Navajo

made her one of their most important holy people. She chose Spider Rock as her home, the awesome peak that rises over eight hundred feet from the depths of Canyon de Chelly. Spider Rock was formed miraculously by swirling, windblown sand that compressed into the red sandstone column.

Elders often told children that if they did not behave themselves, Spider Woman would descend her web ladder, ensnare them, and take them to her home where she would devour them! Children were told that the top of Spider Rock was white with the sun-bleached bones of children who had been captured and eaten.

Yet Spider Woman could also be very kind. Once, a Navajo boy was fleeing an enemy in Canyon de Chelly. Just as the enemy was about to catch him, the young man came upon Spider Rock where he saw a silken cord dangling from the red sandstone tower. Grasping the cord, he quickly scrambled up, barely escaping his pursuer. At the top he met Spider Woman who said she had seen him and had let down the cord. She demonstrated how she spun her web to make the cord. Later, when the young man was certain his enemy was gone, he thanked Spider Woman and descended the magic cord to the canyon floor. He ran home as quickly as possible and told his family how Spider Woman had saved his life.

It was also Spider Woman who many years ago taught Navajo women how to weave upon a loom made by her husband of sky, sun rays, rock crystal, and lightning. To this day, filled with the spirit of Spider Woman, Navajo women weave beautiful rugs and blankets. So strong is the divine presence of Spider Woman, that it is said: "When a baby girl is born to your tribe you shall go and find a spider web which is woven at the mouth of some hole; you must take it and rub it on the baby's hand and arm. Thus, when she grows up she will weave, and her fingers and arms will not tire from the weaving."

Pottery and Baskets

Girls and women also made pottery in the four sacred colors— white, yellow, blue, and black. Most often, they shaped cooking jars, pots, and bowls. These were fragile vessels heated over a fire of piñon wood for several hours to harden the thin clay walls. They also made three kinds of baskets: the water bottle, a tightly woven basket sealed with pine sap; loosely woven wicker baskets for gathering yucca and cactus fruit; and shallow coiled baskets to hold small objects and for use during ceremonies. Only the last kind of basket is made today. Woven of sumac twigs and strips of leaves, the baskets are dyed red, indigo, black, and sometimes yellow. Designs include geometrical or block patterns, and sometimes bands. There is always a narrow exit strip called the "spirit path" where the bands do not come together. If they completed the circle, the Navajo believe they would imprison the spirit of the maker. During a ceremony, the medicine man always places the basket so that the spirit path faces east. Used most often to hold cornmeal porridge in marriage ceremonies, the coiled baskets are now often called wedding baskets.

The lives of the Navajo were clearly defined by work. In

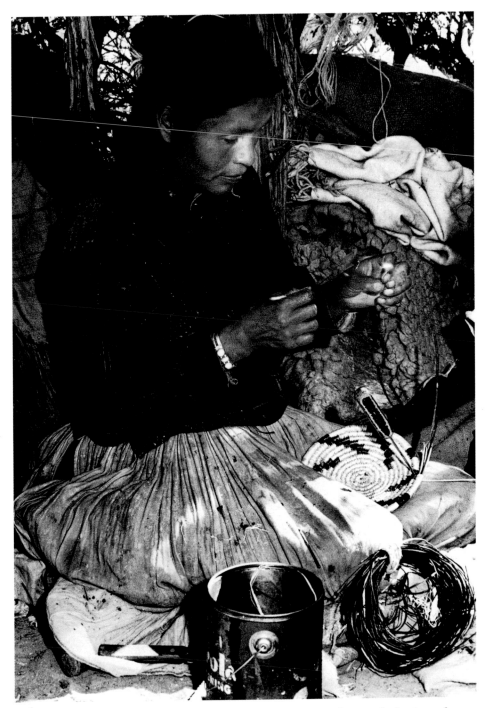

Although best known as weavers, Navajo women also made baskets for storing goods. However, only coiled "wedding baskets" are made today.

addition to feeding and clothing their families, they had to carry firewood for heat and cooking great distances to their hogans. Water was scarce and had to be hauled from creeks or wells located far from home. Yet, living outdoors, they were also filled with a sense of wonder at their lovely surroundings, as expressed in the following song:

> *In beauty I walk.*
> *With the pollen of dawn upon my path*
> *I wander.*
> *With beauty before me, I walk.*
> *With beauty behind me, I walk.*
> *On the trail of morning, I walk.*

Navajo women work hard to provide for their families. A Navajo mother and her two daughters, each holding a lamb, are depicted in this painting by Harrison Begay entitled Treat Me With Love.

Hunting and Warfare

When the Navajo first arrived in the Southwest, the men provided for their families by hunting. They had to travel through the desert and over the mountains in search of large animals, such as pronghorn, elk, mountain sheep, and mountain goats, as well as deer, which was their primary source of meat. Sometimes they journeyed onto the windswept plains to hunt buffalo. They also caught small animals—wood rats, squirrels, rabbits, turkeys, and porcupines.

The Navajo believed that there were proper ways to use everything in the universe to maintain the balance in life—including animals. When killing a deer for meat and skin, it was necessary to show respect for the animal. If wildlife were abused, that is, if more animals were hunted than were needed, game would become scarce and there would be less food and clothing. The Navajo never hunted for sport; they could not conceive of people hunting for fun.

Before the Spanish introduced firearms, men relied on the bow and arrow. They fashioned longbows from mulberry wood. Locust, oak, or maple were also used if mulberry was not available. They made bowstrings from the long sinews in deer legs. For arrows, they chose straight wooden shafts from mountain mahogany, Apache plume, or mulberry. Instead of flint points, they sharpened and fire-hardened the arrow tips, then attached three evenly spaced split feathers to the ends of the shafts. Sometimes, they tipped their arrows with poison from the gallbladder of a deer or

In this Harrison Begay painting, Night Chant, Ceremonial Hunt, *three young men gallop after three deer. Expert hunters, the Navajo respected the animals that provided food for their families.*

with venom from snakes and spiders. They made bow cases and quivers from mountain lion hides, which they believed brought courage and good fortune. For hunting and warfare, men also wielded spears and war clubs, and they protected themselves during battle with hard leather shields, shirts, and hats. They also made knives with flint blades.

Hunters sometimes disguised themselves with masks made from deer or antelope heads and crept up on their prey. Boys and men usually hunted alone or with one or two companions. On longer trips as many as ten men traveled together. Sometimes many people, including women and children, participated in a "surround." The group formed a large circle, then moved toward the center. As the circle tightened, the rabbits or antelope had no means of escape, and the men clubbed them.

Silverwork

In early times, Navajo men were skilled in working leather, wood, and other natural materials into useful household items. They made gourd ladles, wooden spoons, clay pots, parfleches (leather storage pouches), and rope from strips of rawhide. After they acquired horses, they learned to make saddles, bridles, and other riding gear. Over time, men turned their talents to silverwork.

Spanish explorers first introduced the art of silversmithing to the Southwest. Early on, the Navajo used silverwork to adorn their clothes and the bridles of their horses, but they did not practice the craft. They simply acquired horse bridles with silver

This silversmith has carefully hammered pieces of silver into flattened circles, which he strung along a length of rawhide to make a stunning belt.

for precious jewelry. They also hammered coins into silver buttons, which they sewed onto their clothing. The Navajo began to fashion their own silverwork in the 1850s when a Mexican artisan named Nakai Tsosi taught the craft to a Navajo man known as Delgadito. A medicine man and ceremonial singer, Delgadito made his first piece of jewelry from silver coins around 1853. He is believed to be the first silversmith among the Navajo. He taught other Navajos, including his son Red Smith, and so established what has become a tradition among his people.

About this time, Captain Henry L. Dodge, the Indian agent at Fort Defiance, brought in George Carter to teach blacksmithing to the Navajos, who applied the forging skills they learned to their silversmithing. After the Treaty of 1868, the Navajo acquired more specialized tools—anvils, pliers, scissors, and files—which they used to make more intricate objects. Along with buttons, they began to craft earrings, bracelets, belt buckles, and tobacco cases, as well as fancy bridle ornaments. Originally, the Navajo craftsmen acquired their silver by melting down American coins and Mexican pesos.

For hundreds of years, the Navajos had been making jewelry with turquoise and other brightly colored stones. Around 1880, silversmiths living near the Hubbell Trading Post at Ganado, Arizona, began to set the lovely blue stones into their silver jewelry. Navajos who needed money sold, traded, or pawned their jewelry at the post. Many Navajo men—and a few women—have worked for many years to become master silversmiths, and today their exquisite work is admired throughout the world.

4. Beliefs

This painting by Roger Abel Lewis entitled "Blessing of the Veis" depicts the intricate and colorful ceremonies of the Navajo, who believe the physical and spiritual worlds are blended together.

THE NAVAJO HAVE LONG HAD A DEEP-ROOTED AND ABIDING FAITH in nature and their place within the universe. In their language, they have no word for "religion," but their world is permeated with a sense of the supernatural. To them, everything is alive and sacred—not only plants and animals but also stones and soil, wind and rain. Human beings should not dominate nature; they must achieve balance by living in harmony with others and their surroundings, because even the rocks of the mountains feel, think, and speak. Thus, logging strips the earth of its clothes, construction cuts holes into its skin, and mining gouges its flesh. The Navajo believe they live in an interrelated universe in which all things have a proper place—a state of harmony, peace, and prosperity called *hozho*. When the Navajo came into this world, the holy people taught them the right way to conduct themselves—how to provide for themselves, how to build a hogan, how to be a good husband or wife—how to meet the myriad demands of life. The holy people still live in the sacred mountains and often visit the Navajo during their ceremonies and in the course of their daily lives.

Everything in the Navajo universe partakes of either the male or the female. Only when masculine and feminine elements come together is harmony achieved. Whether a man or a woman, the left side of the body is male and the right side is female. The same is true of the hogan. Similarly, Father Sky is male and Mother Earth is female, and life begins where they meet at the horizon. Rather than opposing each other, the two sexes are the complementary halves needed to make all things whole.

In this watercolor by Robert Chee entitled Squaw Dance, men and women dance around the fire at night. The Squaw Dance is among the most common Navajo ceremonies today.

Navajo beliefs are centered around the creation story, in which people gradually emerged from deep within the earth, changing from insectlike people to earth people as they ascended through the different worlds. Each world had to be abandoned because of fighting and other difficulties, and the sins of men and women in the third world are still part of life. The Navajo must also contend with evil and illness that "get in life's way." The Navajo ascended to the Dinetah of the Glittering World, where the holy people, including First Man and First Woman, brought wisdom to guide them. Here, Changing Woman and her twin sons, Monster Slayer and Born for Water, carried out many heroic acts on behalf of the Navajo people. Here, the holy people placed the four sacred mountains in each of the four directions to form the boundaries of Navajo land.

Despite their name, the holy people are not always good—they have the power to help or harm earth people. Although they work to restore order, balance, and harmony to the world, the holy people have not eliminated the monsters of evil and illness. They have done so to teach the Navajo that there is no good without evil, no health without sickness, no riches without poverty, and no abundance without hunger. To this day, the Navajo believe that the poverty, misery, and disease on the reservation are related to wealth, joy, and good health found elsewhere. Ceremonies, called sings or chantways, are held not only to heal or liberate a person from an evil spirit but to encourage rain and bring good fortune, as well as to mark key events in the life of a person or family.

In everyday life, people follow rituals based on these traditional beliefs. Fearful of the holy people, whom they believe have power over their destinies, the Navajos observe taboos to avoid offending them. They avoid trees struck by lightning; they never kill a snake or eat raw meat. Within the hogan, they never step over a sleeping person, and a married man does not speak to his mother-in-law. Yet their lives are not distinguished by fear, but by dignity and good cheer. Laura Gilpin, a well-known photographer of the Navajo, recalled overhearing a man ambling home with his sheep:

Navajo Healing Rite, *a watercolor painted by Jimmy Toddy around 1954, illustrates the importance of elaborate rituals in healing diseases of the body, the mind, and the soul.*

"Suddenly we heard it—a Navajo song—soaring from the woods in the clear, silent mountain air. It was a song of joy, of complete freedom of spirit." The Navajo have always simply taken care to do what was right, so they may journey through life in "the singing way."

Ceremonies

The Navajo have many intricate ceremonies that convey their belief in the world of the spirit. They perform rites, in which a rattle is not used, and chants, in which a rattle accompanies the singing. There are two major kinds of rites: the Blessingway, which keeps people on the path of happiness and wisdom, and the Enemyway, intended to dispel ghosts and discourage evil spirits.

Blessingway ceremonies strengthen harmony by recalling the story of creation and Changing Woman's efforts on behalf of the people. Whenever a hogan is completed, the home is consecrated in a Blessingway ceremony. The Navajo also have Blessingway ceremonies for marriage and travel, as well as hunting and harvesting and many other daily activities. In the Blessingway people give thanks for good health and prosperity as they recall the history of their emergence, particularly the birth of Changing Woman, her rapid coming-of-age, and her union with the Sun, which resulted in the birth of her twins on Huerfano Mountain.

The chants, or chantways, are intended to either maintain or restore good health—both physical and spiritual.

Drypaintings

When disorder occurs in a person's life the Navajo hold healing ceremonies, also called sings or chantways, in which they call upon the holy people to rid the patient of evil, illness, or other misfortune. A special medicine man, called the *hataali*, or singer, comes to the hogan. Before the sing, he fasts, takes a sweat bath, and meditates alone to learn the source of the illness from the spirits. He listens to the night and looks at the stars, eats the herb of enlightenment, and begins to tremble. His whole body shakes and his hands drift over a patch of cornmeal until at last his fingers trace an ancient design that reveals the cause of the illness and the appropriate ritual for its remedy.

The medicine men, who are also artists, create drypaintings, sometimes called sandpaintings. The term *sandpainting* is a misnomer, because medicine men don't really paint, but rather draw. With pollen, cornmeal, and flower petals, as well as ground charcoal from burnt scrub oak and powdered minerals of many brilliant colors—red sandstone, yellow ochre, and white gypsum—they make detailed figures on buckskin or the sand on the floor of the hogan. Some small paintings might be completed in an hour or two. Others might be twenty feet long, requiring as many as a dozen assistants to complete it over the course of the night. Man and painting are joined as the artist works—the colorful powders adhering to his fingers. He comes to understand the meaning of his creation and is given some of its power. The

Pattern and color have become an integral part of Navajo drypaintings and other ritual artwork, as seen in this detail. Often the paintings depict the holy people.

central feature of the healing ceremony. The patient is asked to sit in the center of the sandpainting so the spirits can reach him directly. Outside the hogan, people dance and sing to help the recovery.

The sing may continue for five to nine days, with another drypainting made each evening—drypaintings must be destroyed after each ceremony. There are over five hundred designs, including depictions of the holy people and the constellations, celestial models of a universe in balance. There are also many chants in which people remind themselves that the holy people created an ordered universe and showed the way to live in harmony. Here are the words of one prayer:

Happily I recover
Happily my interior becomes cool
Happily my eyes regain their power
Happily my head becomes cool
Happily my legs regain their power
Happily I hear again!
Happily for me the spell is taken off!
Happily may I walk
In beauty I walk.

Most Navajo ceremonials were developed around 1400, after the Navajo had arrived in the Dinetah and just prior to contact with the Spanish. The fragrance of burning piñon and cedar filling the air, these ceremonials reflect influences from neighboring Apache and Pueblo peoples. The long recitations and drypaintings were oral and visual histories of the work of the holy people in Dinetah. Whether at a performance of a wedding or a healing ceremony, the holy people were called upon to be present. To this day, the Navajo believe that the holy people listen to their songs

Nine Nights Ceremony, *a watercolor made by Jimmy Toddy in 1950, depicts Navajo men and women who have gathered for the evening, with buttes and mesas silhouetted in the background.*

and prayers, not to chastise or forgive their sins, but to help them grow in knowledge so they may achieve a good life. Unlike Western religions, which preach one true path to salvation, the Navajo believe that their lives are filled with uncertainties, risks, and choices, and there are many ways to gain wisdom and to reach old age in a state of harmony.

5. Changing Ways

The Navajo gradually adopted the horse. This family travels in a covered wagon with rubber tires. Before long, many Navajo were acquiring pickup trucks and cars.

THE NAVAJO MAY HAVE LEARNED A GREAT DEAL FROM THE SPANISH, but they were not willing to give up their beliefs. When missionaries tried to force them to attend Mass, the Navajos moved away. However, the Pueblos lived in permanent villages and could not escape Spanish domination. Finally, in 1680, the Pueblos rebelled. The Navajo took part in the Pueblo Revolt, in which the Spanish were driven back toward Mexico. Yet it was not long before the Spanish returned and again conquered the Indian peoples of the Southwest. During the second half of the eighteenth century, Spanish settlers began to move into what is now northwestern New Mexico. The Navajo retaliated with a series of raids, which forced the Spanish to abandon their ranches. Around 1786, Governor Juan Bautista of New Mexico concluded a peace treaty that was kept for the rest of the century. In the early nineteenth century, however, settlers again moved into Navajo territory, igniting more conflict. By the time Americans began arriving in the region, the Navajo had gained a reputation as fierce warriors.

The American government took over the region after the Mexican War in 1848, and the cycle of peace and broken treaties, attacks and reprisals resumed. With no central tribal government, each band of Navajos acted independently and could not be bound by a single treaty. Yet it was most often the Americans who violated the peace agreements. And after seven Navajos, including the famous leader Narbona, lost their lives in a skirmish in 1849, any trust the Navajo may have had was lost.

*A*mong the greatest Navajo leaders was Manuelito, who resisted
American forces invading the ancestral homeland through a series of raids
and retreats. Manuelito remained free until 1866, when he was forced to
surrender or face starvation.

In the 1850s, the Americans built Fort Defiance in the heart of
Navajo country, near present-day Window Rock. They also
established Fort Fauntleroy (later renamed Fort Wingate) in an
effort to control the Navajo. In 1860, about a thousand Navajos,
under the leadership of Manuelito and Barboncito, attacked Fort
Defiance. After the attack failed, the military retaliated by killing
many Navajos, capturing others, and destroying crops and
livestock. Plans were made for the forced removal of the Navajo to

Fort Sumner (known as Bosque Redondo to the Navajo) in eastern New Mexico, a place far from their homes, where they were to be "reformed." During the Navajo War of 1863–1866, Colonel Christopher "Kit" Carson headed "scorched earth" campaigns to make the Mescalero Apaches and the Navajos surrender and accept imprisonment at dismal Bosque Redondo. Red Shirt, as the Navajo call Carson, butchered people and caused terrible starvation over the course of the bitter winter by destroying livestock and food stores. The extreme cruelty of these attacks forced the Navajo to give up and go to Bosque Redondo on the Long Walk, a forced march of 250 miles. It was the first time the Navajo had ever been conquered and sent into exile. Some people living in isolated locations in the west and north had eluded the soldiers, but those bewildered people who went on the Long Walk suffered horribly.

Under the leadership of General James H. Carleton, the initiative was intended to educate and transform the Navajo into peaceful farmers, but it failed miserably. To this day, the Navajo remember how cruelly their ancestors were treated during the years of confinement. People were hungry and sick, and conditions were so bad that the Navajo lived in holes dug in the ground. Hundreds of people died. The imprisoned Navajo called upon the holy people to release them, which finally happened under the terms of the Treaty of 1868.

This brutal episode in their history began to unite the Navajo as a people. For the first time they began to view themselves as a

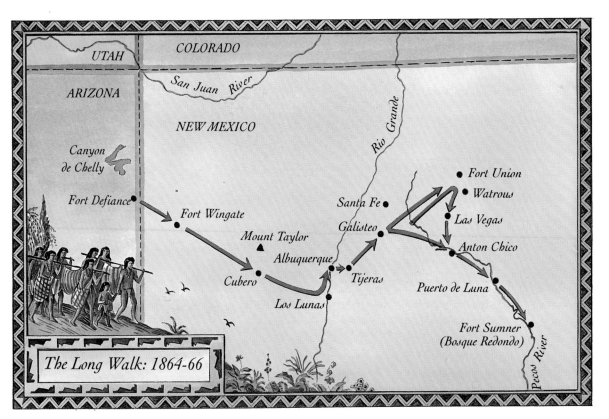

The Long Walk: 1864–66

D uring the Long Walk the Navajo were driven far away to unfamiliar land. Exhausted and hungry, they weren't sure where they were going and if they would be ever be able to return to their homeland.

nation. The Treaty of 1868 also created a huge reservation of 3.5 million acres in New Mexico and Arizona. Men, women, and children straggled home with just five thousand sheep remaining from the nearly five hundred thousand they had had before the war with the United States. However, although the reservation was only a remnant of their former territory, unlike so many other native peoples, the Navajo were not relocated to an unfamiliar place. They had come home and because the Americans considered the land of little economic value, they were left alone in their isolated region. Over time, they were able to expand their territory. Had the United States government known of the mineral riches under the land, the reservation would not have grown to its present impressive size. At the time, however, officials thought the land was little more than parched desert.

Following their return from Bosque Redondo, the Navajo soon brought their herds of sheep, horses, and cattle back up to the numbers of the 1840s. Returning to self-sufficient lives as farmers, herders, and weavers, they generally fared better than other Native American peoples. Wool, hides, and meat were sent to market; rugs and blankets were woven and sold at trading posts. Since there were few towns in the region, trading posts, such as Hubbell Trading Post at Ganado and Goulding's Trading Post near Monument Valley, became key places to sell weaving and silverwork during frontier times. From the 1870s to the present, trading posts have dotted the reservation. Like the hub of a wheel, they have historically been the economic centers of different

*R*oman Hubbell, owner of Hubbell Trading Post, talks to a Navajo customer. Located in the heart of the Navajo reservation, the trading post is now a national landmark.

regions on the reservation. Traders were viewed as legendary figures—rugged pioneers with a keen business sense—and they generally treated the Navajos fairly. The Navajo loved the game of trading and had great respect for those who made the best deal. People brought in wool at shearing time and perhaps a few cattle at the annual fall roundup, along with stacks of hides, bags of piñon nuts, woven blankets, and handmade jewelry. Christian missionaries moved onto the reservation, building schools and hospitals—and pressuring the Navajo to abandon their deeply held beliefs. The Treaty of 1868 arrogantly stated, "In order to

As much as children were eager to learn about the world beyond the reservation, they did not want to leave their homes to attend boarding schools. Even today many children must travel to school by bus up to forty miles each way.

insure the civilization of the Indians entering into this treaty, the necessity of education is admitted." This compulsory education required young people to move away from home and to abandon their way of life. Few Navajos attended these government schools, and those who did often ran away from these attempts to "civilize" them. The Navajo accepted the traders who exchanged goods, but despised the educators and missionaries who wanted to destroy their heritage and give them nothing in return.

The Navajo suffered dearly—in the most painful experience since the Long Walk—when they were required to reduce the number of their livestock in the 1930s. As early as 1894, government officials had noted overgrazing. In 1914, a priest at St. Michael's Mission again raised concerns about too many sheep and cattle. It was also noted that young children were often responsible for pasturing the herds. In the late 1920s, the federal government required herd reduction to ease the threat of soil erosion. Navajos were forced to slaughter half their sheep. They were especially outraged that government officials allowed thousands of sheep to die in holding stalls. To this day, the Navajo bitterly dispute the need for reduction, and it has taken a long time for their flocks to recover to their former size. Sam Ahkeah, Navajo Tribal Council chair from 1946 to 1954, called livestock reduction "the most devastating experience in Navajo history since the imprisonment at Fort Sumner from 1864 to 1868."

In the early twentieth century, federal officials authorized the creation of five Navajo agencies, which slowed the development of a central government by dividing the reservation into regions and adding more bureaucracy. The Court of Indian Offenses was also established with chapters in each community. When the Metalliferous Minerals Leasing Act of 1918 was passed, followed by the General Leasing Act of 1920, the Navajo reservation was opened to exploitation by mining interests. The discovery of oil on

These sheep are slowly making their way up a hillside in search of tender plants. Flocks like these were a rare sight after the mismanaged livestock reduction of the 1920s.

the reservation in 1921 led to the formation of the Navajo Tribal Council and a central government authorized to grant leases. The era of isolation was over. A controversial period began in which the Navajo people debated the mining and drilling, which brought badly needed capital to the impoverished reservation but also harmed their cherished land.

6. New Ways

Three generations of a Navajo family—
grandfather, father, and son—pose near their
home on the reservation. Today's generation
blends modern attitudes with a traditional
approach to life.

THE NAVAJOS HAVE NOT VANISHED. ON THE CONTRARY, FROM 1868 to the early 1900s, the population of around 15,000 people doubled and has continued to grow steadily throughout the twentieth century. With a population of over 200,000 people in 1999, the Navajo Nation is the largest Native American tribe and among the fastest growing of any ethnic group in the United States. Fully three-quarters of the population is under twenty-eight years old. Most people live on the reservation within the embrace of the four sacred mountains. Covering an area of about 27,000 square miles, the Navajo Nation is the largest reservation in North America—slightly larger than the state of West Virginia. The reservation includes a large portion of northeastern Arizona, part of northwestern New Mexico, and a small portion of southeastern Utah.

The Diné had a distinct culture in the Southwest long before the Spanish arrived in North America and long before the United States became established. The government of the United States entered into treaties with the Navajo Nation, and over the years both the Congress and the Supreme Court have acknowledged the inherent right of the Navajo to govern themselves. The Navajo lived in their homeland long before the states of Arizona and New Mexico were established. Today, the Navajo have maintained the flame of traditional life, yet like their ancestors, they have also continued to be remarkably flexible in responding to change. A sense of identity as a nation has also arisen in recent years as people have become aware of their common heritage.

*T*heir grandmother speaks only Navajo, but these girls not only speak English, they have embraced many aspects of popular culture.

Navajo Language

Navajo is a fascinating language. During World War II, United States military leaders needed a code to keep the Japanese from reading secret messages. They turned to the Navajo whose spoken language is so complex that it could not be easily deciphered. So, the 382nd Platoon was formed entirely of Navajo volunteers, who became known as the Code Talkers—eventually four hundred men served in this unit. They made up new names for weapons and war materials for which there was no Navajo word. For instance, dive-bombers were called *ginitsoh,* which means "sparrow hawk." *Beshlo,* or "iron fish," became the word for submarine. The Navajo word for "potato" meant "hand grenade" and "whale" meant "battleship." The Navajo word for "our mother" was used to signify the United States, and clan names were used for military units. The Navajo Code Talkers were so successful that the Japanese could not break the code throughout the entire war. The Code Talkers were honored as great American heroes for the crucial role they played in the Pacific.

Today, unlike many native peoples who are struggling to recover their language, the Navajo have never stopped speaking their native tongue. Scholars have also prepared dictionaries and textbooks for written Navajo, which is now taught in public schools on the reservation. You may wish to learn a few words of Navajo yourself. Because of the accent marks, these words may appear to be a challenge, but if you follow the key, you'll find that the pronunciation is not too difficult. These examples are based on the *Conversational Navajo Dictionary* by Garth Wilson and the *Navajo-English Dictionary* by Leon Wall and William Morgan.

The short vowels are pronounced as follows:

a	as in father
e	as in west
i	as in sit
o	as in low

The long, or doubled, vowels are pronounced the same, but the sounds are held a little longer:

aa	as in say "*aah*"
ee	as in yeah
ii	as in see
oo	as in *oh*

The diphthongs (combined vowels) are pronounced as follows:

ai	as in my
ao	as in cow
ei	as in say
oi	as in chewy

Some Navajo words are nasalized, that is, the sound passes through the nose instead of the mouth, as in the French word *non*. The vowels of these words are indicated here in boldface type. For example, the word for deer is *biih* with a nasal sound, so the word is printed as "**biih**."

An accent mark following a syllable indicates stress. Navajo vowels may be spoken in a high tone, indicated by an accent above the vowel. Sometimes the l is aspirated with air expelled on either side of the tongue. Because this is a difficult sound for English speakers, you may simply pronounce this letter as an "l."

Here are some examples of words spoken by Navajo people, some of which are especially important in their world. Others are everyday words that show just how much you have in common with Navajo children.

boy	ashkii
brother	ánaaí (older)
brother	átsilí (younger)
children	álchíní
corn	naadáá'
coyote	ma'ii
deer	biih
dog	lééchaa'í
earth	nahosdzáán; also ni'
father	azhé'é
feather	ats'os
fire	ko'
fish	lóó'
forest	tsintah
friend	alah (of the opposite sex)
friend	ak'is (of the same sex)

frog	ch'al
girl	at'ééd
goat	tl'ízí
hello	yá'át'ééh (also means "It is good.")
home	hooghan
horse	líí'
house	kin (also trading post)
mother	amá
mountain	dzil
no	dooda
rabbit	gah
rug	diyogi
school	ólta'
sheep	dibé
silver	béésh ligaii
singer	hataali (medicine man)
sister	ádí (older)
sister	adeezhi (younger)
sky	yá
smoke	lid
sun	jóhonaa'eí
turquoise	dootl'i'izhii
water	tó
wool	aghaa'
yes	aoo'

Walking in Beauty

Today, the Navajo have united to protect their interests. As a people, they are asserting their political rights as well as sustaining their traditional ways—although it is difficult to be a nation within a nation. The Navajo Tribal Code directs the leaders "to work out the relationship of its nation to the United States and the surrounding states." Yet the nature of this relationship has not been clearly determined—the Navajo wish to be recognized as their own sovereign nation, while state and federal authorities are unwilling to grant full independence to the Navajo Nation.

To a traveler on the reservation, the life on Dinetah may not seem to have changed much over the hundred years. Hogans are scattered across the sprawling landscape—rising over stretches of pale green sage, tucked in among the red rocks, and nestled in the pine woods. However, most are now made of two-by-fours and plywood. Many homes are without electricity and running water. Small frame houses are also clustered at the edge of the towns— Tuba City, Kayenta, Chinle, and Window Rock—along with a gas station, the post office, a school, and the chapter house. A trading post may also be situated at a desert crossroads or along a lonely strip of asphalt highway. Although the Navajo Nation has its own police force and a public health service, including clinics and hospitals, most people live too far away from towns to receive immediate help.

Children once herded the sheep, but they are now in school— sometimes traveling as far as forty miles each way on lumbering yellow school buses. So, grandmothers have taken over the

Many Navajo still live in hogans. Whether made of logs or lumber, the hogans are scattered over the reservation—from deep in Canyon de Chelly to the sands and sage of Monument Valley.

arduous task of herding the sheep. Because of thin grazing land, they must wander with their sheep, with the help of alert herding dogs, over great distances. Most of the old women speak no English, but their grandchildren sound and act like other American children.

A generous people who take care of each ·other, the Navajo value harmony and peace more than personal wealth. Despite widespread poverty, they have a lively sense of humor and enjoy the company of others. A spiritual people, the Navajo continue to follow their traditional beliefs. As always, they honor nature and "walk in beauty."

More About

the Navajo

Time Line

1000s–1500s After a long period of migration from the Northwest, the Navajo settle in what is now the American Southwest

1500s–1800s Navajo share the Southwest with several Indian peoples, including the Hopis, as well as the Spanish and the Mexicans

1680 Navajo take part in the Pueblo Revolt that drives the Spanish from the Southwest

1692 Spanish reoccupy the region, except for the Hopi lands

1848 Mexican War ends with the Treaty of Guadalupe Hidalgo; Mexico cedes the Southwest to the United States

1849 Navajos skirmish with United States troops after their leader Narbona is killed by the Americans

1849–1851 During the California Gold Rush, prospectors cross Navajo lands; the United States wars against the Navajo people

1861 Treaty between the Navajos and the United States promises friendship and peace

1863–1866 The Navajo War. In 1864 Colonel Kit Carson and U.S. soldiers destroy Navajo livestock and crops, and force the Navajo on the Long Walk, a 250-mile journey to Fort Sumner, New Mexico. Many men, women, and children perish during the grueling march

1864–1868 Navajos are imprisoned at Fort Sumner under deplorable conditions

1868 Under the Treaty of 1868, the Navajos are released from Fort Sumner and a reservation is established for them in northwestern New Mexico

1871 Navajo and Hopi children are removed from their homes and forced to attend government schools

1878, 1882 Navajo reservation expands into Arizona

1909 U.S. Geological Survey discovers an estimated eight billion tons of coal under Black Mesa on the Navajo reservation

1921 Oil is discovered on the Navajo reservation

1923 First Navajo Tribal Council formed by the Department of the Interior to authorize an Indian agent to sign leases for mineral rights

1924 Native Americans born in the United States, including Navajos, are declared citizens

1932 Ten-year period of livestock reduction begins on the Navajo reservation

1941–1945 Navajo people serve in the United States military during World War II; among them are the famed Code Talkers

1948 Arizona and New Mexico, the last states to do so, grant Native Americans, including the Navajo, the right to vote in elections

1950 Navajo-Hopi Rehabilitation Act authorizes $90 million for construction of wells, roads, schools, and health clinics

1954 Uranium begins to be mined on the Navajo reservation

1965 Navajos establish the Office of Navajo Economic Opportunity (ONEO) and appoint Peter MacDonald as executive director

1966 Navajo-Hopi Land Settlement Act becomes law, leading to a bitter and ongoing land dispute between the two tribes

1969 The Navajo officially call themselves the Navajo Nation; Navajo Community College, now Diné College, is founded

1981 The Navajo Nation opens a Washington, D.C., office to lobby on behalf of their people and to monitor legislation affecting all Native Americans

1985 Twelve-million-dollar cleanup project for uranium tailings left from a uranium mill built in 1954

Notable People

Armijo (active mid-1800s) was a prominent farmer and a leader in the Navajo War of 1863–1866. Adopting the name of Manuel Armijo, he became the governor of New Mexico when it was still part of Mexican territory. The Navajo leader lived on a farm in the Chuska foothills of New Mexico. Although he consistently advocated peace between American Indians and settlers, he raided settlers along with Navajo leader Manuelito when hostilities erupted in the 1860s. After a long struggle with American forces, Armijo finally surrendered in April 1864. He and his followers were relocated along with other Navajos to Fort Sumner in New Mexico. In 1868, he was among the signers of a treaty establishing the Navajo reservation in Arizona and New Mexico.

Barboncito (about 1820–1871), a brother of Delgadito, was born in the heart of Navajo country at Canyon de Chelly in present-day northeastern Arizona. He grew up to become a ceremonial singer and a war chief during the Navajo War of 1863–1866. He signed a treaty with Alexander W. Doniphan during the Mexican War in 1846, agreeing to peaceful relations with white settlers. However, in 1860, after soldiers killed Navajo horses in a dispute over grazing lands, Barboncito joined the Navajo leader Manuelito in an attack on Fort Defiance. Two years later, Barboncito and his brother Delgadito sought peace with General James H. Carleton. But in 1863, when ordered to relocate to Bosque Redondo in New Mexico, the brothers again allied with Manuelito in rebellion.

Captured at Canyon de Chelly in 1864 by troops under the command of Kit Carson, Barboncito was forced to relocate to Bosque Redondo with other Navajos and Mescalero Apaches. Confronted with atrocious living conditions, he and about five hundred followers escaped and rejoined Manuelito. He again surrendered in November 1866, along with twenty-one followers. Barboncito was one of the signers of the Treaty of 1868 establishing the Navajo reservation. Confined to the reservation, he died three years later.

Delgadito (about 1830–1870), a medicine man and a ceremonial singer, took part in the Navajo War (1863–1866). He is also believed to be the first silversmith among the Navajo. In the 1850s, Nakai Tsosi, a Mexican artisan, taught the craft to Delgadito. About the same time, Captain Henry L. Dodge, the Indian agent at Fort Defiance, brought in George Carter to teach blacksmithing to the Navajos. Around 1853, Delgadito made his first piece of jewelry from silver coins. He taught other Navajos, including his son Red Smith, and so established a tradition among his people.

Delgadito and his brother Barboncito led five hundred warriors in alliance with the leader Manuelito. After Kit Carson's campaign to destroy Navajo livestock and grain, the two brothers sued for peace in 1863. They agreed to settle near Fort Wingate but were forced to resettle at Bosque Redondo. Delgadito was one of the signers of the Treaty of 1868, which allowed the Navajo to return to their homeland, although restricting them to the reservation.

Henry Chee Dodge (about 1857–1947) was born at Fort Defiance, the son of a Navajo-Jemez mother named Bisnayanchi. His father was believed to be Henry L. Dodge, the white agent to the Navajo. His stepfather passed away when he was an infant and his mother died in 1864 during Kit Carson's brutal campaign. Adopted by an old man and his granddaughter, Dodge accompanied them on the Long Walk. Returning to Fort Defiance in 1868, he was reunited with his Navajo aunt who was married to Perry H. Williams, an agency employee. Williams taught Dodge to speak English, and later, at the Fort Defiance Indian School, he learned to read and write English as well. He

Henry Chee Dodge

R. C. Gorman

soon became the official interpreter for the Navajo.

In 1885, Dodge succeeded Manuelito as leader of the Navajo people. Appointed by the Bureau of Indian Affairs, he negotiated with federal officials but was not recognized by the various bands that had their own leaders. In 1890, he became a partner in a trading post and invested in livestock, both ventures proving successful. In 1923, Dodge became the first chairman of the Navajo Tribal Council and served in that position for over ten years. He was re-elected in 1942 and again in 1946 but died a year later. Dodge was influential in transforming the tribe into a modern organization. He promoted economic development among his people and also encouraged traditional arts and beliefs.

R. C. Gorman (1932–   ), noted Native American artist, was born on the Navajo reservation at Chinle, Arizona. Descended from drypainters, weavers, and silversmiths on both sides of his family, Gorman is the son of the celebrated artist Carl Nelson Gorman. Raised in a traditional manner, Gorman lived in a hogan and herded sheep with his grandmother. Much of his early work honored women as they cared for their families, nursing babies, raising corn, and cooking at the fire. Gorman studied art at Northern Arizona University and Mexico City College. Having received numerous awards and honors for his traditional paintings, he lives and works at his home in Taos, New Mexico.

Hosteen Klah (1867–1937), a prominent medicine man, also became a skilled weaver. He was born into a family of well-known leaders (his great-grandfather was Narbona) during the Navajo exile at Bosque Redondo. As an infant, he returned with his family to their home country. During his childhood, Klah (which means "left-handed") herded sheep and learned weaving from his grandmother. Apprenticed to several relatives who were medicine men, he studied for twenty-six years before holding his first Yeibichai Ceremony in 1917. He also worked with Mary Cabot Wheelwright and Franc Newcomb to record many of his songs and drypaintings.

In 1920, he caused an uproar among the Navajo when he wove a rug with a design based on one of the drypaintings of the Yeibichai Ceremony. But the use of drypainting themes has since become popular in weavings. Klah gained an international reputation as a weaver and had his rugs exhibited at two world's fairs. He spent many years training Beaal Begay as an apprentice, but Begay died unexpectedly in 1931. When Klah died a few years later, many Navajo prayers and rituals were lost forever.

Ganado Mucho (about 1809–1893), the son of a Navajo woman and a Hopi man, grew up to become a successful rancher near present-day Klagetoh, south of Canyon de Chelly, in northeastern Arizona. He also became the leader of a band of Navajo. In the 1850s, he was accused of cattle theft by white settlers, due to the size of his herd. But he and other Navajo ranchers signed an agreement to return any livestock that wandered into their herd.

During the Navajo War, Ganado Mucho sought peace. When that was not possible, he and his followers eluded Kit Carson. Finally, in 1865, he led his band to Bosque Redondo. He lost his son and two daughters to slave raids by Mexicans and Ute Indians. One of the signers of the Treaty of 1868 allowing the Navajo to return to their ancestral homeland, Ganado rebuilt his herd and resumed his role as peacemaker between the Navajo and the settlers.

Herrero Grande (active mid-1800s) learned the craft of blacksmithing from George Carter while living at Fort Defiance in the 1850s. Just as Delgadito was admired for his silverwork, Herrero gained fame for his knife blades, bits, and other bridle parts.

After a council with white officials at Fort Fauntleroy in 1861, Herrero was elected principal leader of the Navajo people. Refusing the order of relocation, he went into hiding but surrendered in 1864, taking his band as ordered on the Long Walk to exile at Bosque Redondo. Thereafter, he served as a peacemaker, meeting with Manuelito on behalf of General James H. Carleton in 1865. However, he was unable to convince the great leader to surrender. Along with other leaders, Herrero Grande signed the Treaty of 1868, which established the Navajo reservation.

Manuelito (about 1818–1894) rose to prominence as a great warrior and married the daughter of the war chief Narbona. Later, he acquired a second wife in a raid on a Mexican settlement.

During the winter of 1846, Manuelito eluded United States troops in Canyon de Chelly. Navajo leaders signed treaties with the United States that year and in 1849 but remained militant until the 1860s. The Navajos fought U.S. soldiers over their ancestral pasturelands near Fort Defiance. After the soldiers killed Navajo horses and the warriors raided army herds, Manuelito was chosen to be leader. Manuelito continued the raids, and in retaliation the soldiers destroyed his home, crops, and livestock. In 1860, Manuelito and his warriors attacked and nearly overtook Fort Defiance. Colonel Edward Canby pursued him, but Manuelito and his warriors repelled him in a series of raids. In 1861, Manuelito and other leaders agreed to work for peace, but raids and skirmishes continued. In 1863, Kit Carson embarked on a campaign in which he destroyed Navajo homes, crops, and livestock.

Manuelito resisted to the end. Finally in November, 1866, he appeared at Fort Wingate with twenty-three half-starved warriors. When the Navajo people returned to their homeland, Manuelito was named principal chief in 1870, as well as chief of police in 1872. He was succeeded as chief by Henry Chee Dodge in 1885.

Luci Tapahonso

Luci Tapahonso (1953–   ) is a well-known writer and poet. Originally from Shiprock, New Mexico, she first told many of her stories in Navajo. Passed down over the generations, these stories weave together a rich texture of place and people, emphasizing the strength of family ties.

She is the author of four books of poetry: *Seasonal Woman* (1982), *One More Shiprock Night* (1981), *A Breeze Swept Through* (1987), and *Sáanii Dahataal, The Women Are Singing* (1993). Tapahonso has also published a children's book, *Navajo ABC: A Diné Alphabet Book*, and a collection of poems and stories entitled *Blue Horses Rush In*. She is an associate professor of English at the University of Kansas in Lawrence.

Peterson Zah

Peterson Zah (1937–   ), born in Low Mountain, New Mexico, was elected the first president of the Navajo Nation. He attended Arizona State University on a basketball scholarship, graduating in 1963 with a degree in education. He returned to Window Rock, Arizona, where he taught carpentry and worked in various social and legal service programs to help people on the reservation.

In 1982, he won a victory over Peter MacDonald for the chairmanship of the Navajo Tribal Council. During his campaign, he emphasized economic development. After the completion of his four-year term, he became a fundraiser and later a consultant for school materials on Navajo culture and history. After the Navajo Nation reorganized, Peterson Zah was elected president of the Navajo Nation—the first person to hold this new position.

Glossary

Athapaskan Language group to which the Navajo language belongs

Blessingway General name for a group of ceremonies that bring order and happiness in life

brush circle A temporary shelter used when hunting or setting up a sheep camp or as a first home for newlyweds

Changing Woman Mythical person from whom the Navajo people were created

chantway A ceremony for healing. Also called a sing

Diné Navajo name for themselves, meaning "person"

Dinetah Navajo name for their homeland in Arizona and New Mexico

First Man Mythical figure who, with First Woman, emerged from the underworld into the Dinetah

First Woman Mythical figure who, with First Man, rose from the underworld into the Dinetah

hogan A house, most often with six or eight sides, a domed roof, and a single door always facing east

holy people Invisible spiritual beings who show the Navajo how to properly conduct themselves in everyday life

Kinaaldá A ceremony for girls when they come of age, so they might always "walk in beauty"

Long Walk The exile of the Navajo in which they were forced to march 250 miles from their homeland to Bosque Redondo

ramada A windbreak or shelter that resembles an open porch made of branches and brush. Also called a shade

reservation An area of land owned by an Indian tribe, but under supervision of the United States government

shade A brush shelter that resembles an open porch. Also called a ramada

sing A sacred ceremony. Also called a chantway

singer Navajo medicine man; one who conducts a ceremony

Spider Woman Mythical person who gave power to Monster Slayer and Born for Water to search for their father the Sun

Tribal Council The legal governing body for the Navajo Nation, with seventy-four members elected by people on the reservation

Further Information

Readings

Many fine books have been written about the Navajo. Among them, the following titles were consulted in researching and writing *The Navajo*:

Arthur, Claudeen et al., *Between Sacred Mountains: Navajo Stories and Lessons from the Land*. Tucson, AZ: Sun Tracks and University of Arizona Press, 1984.

Bailey, Garrick, and Bailey, Roberta Glenn. *A History of the Navajos: The Reservation Years*. Santa Fe: School of American Research Press, 1986.

Blomberg, Nancy J. *Navajo Textiles: The William Randolph Hearst Collection*. Tucson, AZ: University of Arizona Press, 1988.

Curtis, Edward S. *The North American Indian: Being a Series of Volumes Picturing and Describing the Indians of the United States and Alaska*. Volume 1. New York: Johnson Reprint Corp., 1970.

Dutton, Bertha P. *Navahos and Apaches: the Athabascan Peoples*. Englewood Cliffs, N.J.: Prentice-Hall, 1975.

Gilpin, Laura. *The Enduring Navaho*. Austin: University of Texas Press, 1968.

Hirschfelder, Arlene, and Kreipe de Montano, Martha. *The Native American Almanac: A Portrait of Native America Today*. New York: Prentice Hall, 1993.

Iverson, Peter. *The Navajo Nation*. Albuquerque: University of New Mexico Press, 1981.

Jacka, Jerry, and Jacka, Lois Essary. *Enduring Traditions: Art of the Navajo*. Flagstaff, AZ: Northland Publishing, 1994.

Johansen, Bruce E., and Grinde, Donald A. Jr. *The Encyclopedia of Native American Biography*. New York: Henry Holt, 1997.

Kluckhohn, Clyde, Hill, W.W., and Kluckhohn, Lucy Wales. *Navaho Material Culture*. Cambridge, MA: Harvard University Press, 1971.

Langer, Howard J., ed. *American Indian Quotations*. Westport, CT: Greenwood Press, 1996.

Lindig, Wolfgang, and Teiwes, Helga. *Navajo*. New York: Facts on File, 1993.

Minear, Tish, and Limon, Janet. *Discover Native America: Arizona, Colorado,*

New Mexico, Utah. New York: Hippocrene Books, 1995.

O'Bryan, Aileen. Smithsonian Institution. Bureau of American Ethnology. Bulletin 163. *The Diné: Origin Myths of the Navaho Indians*. Washington, DC: United States Government Printing Office, 1956.

Sturtevant, William C. ed., Ortiz, Alfonso, volume editor. *Handbook of North American Indians*. v. 9–10 Southwest. Washington: Smithsonian Institution, 1983.

Shanks, Ralph C., and Shanks, Lisa Woo. *The North American Indian Travel Guide*. Petaluma, CA: Costano Books, 1993.

Sundberg, Lawrence D. *Dinétah: An Early History of the Navajo People*. Santa Fe, NM: Sunstone Press, 1995.

Wall, C. Leon, et al. *Navajo-English Dictionary*. New York: Hippocrene Books, 1994.

Washburn, Dorothy K. *Living in Balance: The Universe of the Hopi, Zuni, Navajo, and Apache*. Philadelphia: University of Pennsylvania Museum of Archaeology and Anthropology, 1995.

Willink, Roseann Sandoval, and Zolbrod, Paul G. *Weaving a World: Textiles and the Navajo Way of Seeing*. Santa Fe: University of New Mexico Press, 1997.

Wilson, Garth. *Conversational Navajo Dictionary*. Blanding, UT: Conversational Navajo Publications, 1994.

Witherspoon, Gary. *Navajo Kinship and Marriage*. Chicago: University of Chicago Press, 1975.

Yazzie, Ethelou, ed. *Navajo History*. Many Farms, AZ: Navajo Community College Press, 1971.

Young people who wish to learn more about the Navajo will enjoy these excellent books for children:

Armstrong, Nancy M. *Navajo Long Walk*. New York: Scholastic, 1996.

Bonvillain, Nancy. *The Navajos: People of the Southwest*. Brookfield, CT: Millbrook Press, 1995.

Cohlene, Terri. *Turquoise Boy*. Vero Beach, FL: Rourke, 1990.

Doherty, Craig A., and Doherty, Katherine M. *The Apaches and Navajos*. New York: Franklin Watts, 1989.

Erdoes, Richard. *The Native Americans: Navajos*. New York: Sterling Publishing, 1978.

Hood, Flora. *Living in Navajoland*. New York: G.P. Putnam's Sons, 1970.

Sneve, Virginia Driving Hawk. *The Navajos*. Needham, MA: Silver Burdett Ginn, 1996.

————. *The Navajos*. New York: Holiday House, 1993.

Stan, Susan. *The Navajo*. Vero Beach, FL: Rourke Publications, 1989.

Wood, Leigh Hope. *The Navajo Indians*. New York: Chelsea House, 1991.

Websites

Over the past few years, Native Americans have established themselves on the Internet. Here are some of the best and most interesting websites to visit for more information about the Navajo Nation and other native peoples.

The American Indian Link Exchange
http://www.cris.com/~misterg/award/whoshot.htm
Diné College
http://crystal.ncc.cc.nm.us/main2.html
Dineh Alliance
http://www.primenet.com/~dineh/index.html
First Nations: Histories
http://www.dickshovel.com/Compacts.html
FirstNations.Com
http://www.firstnations.com
Index of Native American Resources on the Internet
http://hanksville.phast.umass.edu/misc/NAresources.html
Native American Sites
http://www.pitt.edu/~lmitten/indians.html
Native Americans
http://www.americanwest.com/pages/indians.htm
NativeWeb
http://www.nativeweb.org
Navajo Nation
http://crystal.ncc.cc.nm.us/~vino/NN
Tseyi Heritage Cultural Center
http://crystal.ncc.cc.nm.us/~vino/NN/Tseyi/tseyi.html

Organizations

Canyon de Chelly National Monument
P. O. Box 588
Chinle, AZ 86503
(520) 674-5436 or (520) 674-5500

Diné College (formerly Navajo Community College) Ned Hatathlii Center
Tsaile, AZ 86556
(520) 724-6600

Hubbell Trading Post National Historical Site
P. O. Box 150
Ganado, AZ 86505
(520) 755-3475

Monument Valley Navajo Tribal Park
P. O. Box 360289
Monument Valley, UT 84536
(801) 727-3353 or (801) 727-3287

Navajo Arts & Crafts Enterprise
P. O. Drawer A
Window Rock, AZ 86515
(520) 871-4090 or (520) 871-4095

Navajo Nation Council Chambers
P. O. Box 1400
Window Rock, AZ 86515
(520) 871-6417

Navajo National Monument
Hwy 564
Kayenta, AZ
(520) 672-2366

Navajo Tourism Department
P. O. Box 663
Window Rock, AZ 86515
(520) 871-6436 or (520) 871-7371
Fax (520) 871-7381

Navajo Tribal Museum
P. O. Box 9000
Window Rock, AZ 85615
(520) 871-6673

Rainbow Natural Bridge
Navajo Parks and Recreation Department
P. O. Box 9000
Window Rock, AZ 86515
(520) 871-6647 or (520) 871-7307

Ramah Navajo Chapter
P. O. Box 6008
Bernalillo, NM 87004
(505) 867-3317

St. Michael's Historical Museum
P. O. Box 680
St. Michaels, AZ 86511
(520) 871-4171

Index

Page numbers for illustrations are in **boldface**.

agriculture, 19, 20, **22**, 54–55
American government, 90–94
ancestors, 17-19
animal skins, 19, 58–60
animals, 11-12, 20, 25, 33
Apaches, 17, 19
Arizona, 17, 19, 21, 75, 92, 102
Armijo, Manuel, 114
Athapaskan language, 17

balance, male and female, 78–80
Barboncito, 91, 114
baskets, 68, **69**
Begay, Harrison, **13**, **70**, **72**
beliefs, 10, **13**, 23-25, 34, 78–87
biographies, 114–119
birth, 46
Black World, 10
blacksmiths, 75
blankets, 20, 40, 62–66, 94
Blessingway ceremonies, 34, 38–39, 51, 82
Blue World, 11–12
Born for Water, 15, 80
Bosque Redondo (Fort Sumner), 91–92, 114
bow and arrow, 71–73
bread, 57, 58
brush circles, 26, 42, **43**
burial, 52

Canyon de Chelly, 21, **22–23**, **35**, **52–53**, 67, **109**, 114, 118
Carson, Kit, 92, 114, 115, 117, 118
Carter, George, 75, 115, 117
cattle, 20, 26, 33, 94

ceremonies, 15, 34, 38–39, **43**, 49, 68, **76–77**, **79**, 80, 82
ceremonies, origin, 85-86
Changing Woman, 15, 49, 80, 82chantways, 80, 82, 83
childhood, 46–49
children, **13**, 46, **50**, **96**
children, work of, 19, 47, 49, 97
chores, 49
clans, 30
clothing, 19, 58–61, **59**, **61**
clothing adornments, 75
Code Talkers, 104
cooking, 55–58, **56**
corn, 11, 14, 54–55, **56**, 58, 66
corn pollen, 34, 46, 51
cornmeal, 51, 55
courtship, 49–51
Coyote the Trickster, 11, 12, 14
cradleboards, 46–47, **48**
crafts, 73
creation story, 10–17, **28–29**, 34, 66–68, 80, 82
crops, 14, 19
Crossing of the Waters, 12
culture, 10, 19, 33, 102, **103**

dancing, **79**
death, 14, 51–52
Delgadito, 75, 114, 115
desert, 21
designs, 65–66
Diné culture, 19, 102
Dinetah, 21, 80, 108
Dodge, Captain Henry L., 75, 115
Dodge, Henry Chee, 115–116, **115**, 118

drypaintings (sandpaintings), 83–87, **84**, 117
dugouts, 34–35
dyes, 62–66

education, **13**, 95–97, **96**, 108–109
Enemyway, 82

families, 30, 34, 39–40, 42–43, **50, 70**, **100–101**
family life, 46–52
farming, 19, 30, **52–53**, 54–55, 94
fertility symbol. *See* corn pollen
fire, 14, 38
First Man and First Woman, 11, 12, 14, 34, 80
food, 53–58,
Fort Defiance, 90–91
Fort Sumner (Bosque Redondo), 91–92, 114

gambling customs, 41
geography, 10, 102
Gilpin, Laura, 81–82
Glittering World, 14–17, 27
goats, 20, 43, 62
Gobernado Canyon, 17
Gorman, Carl Nelson, 10, 116
Gorman, R. C., 116, **116**
government, 30, 98–99
Grande, Herrero, 117–118

handiwork, 73
hataali (medicine man), 83
healing ceremony, **81**, 85
herbal medicines, 54
herding, 30, 33
hides, tanning, 58–60
hogans, 14, 17, 26, **28–29**, **31**, 33–43, **35, 36, 37, 39**, 51–52, 81, 82, 108, **109**
holy people, 42, 49, 51, 78–80, 83, 85, 86–87, 92
homeland, **18**, 21, 23

horses, 20, 26, 33, 51, **72**, 94
Hubbell Trading Post, **95**
hunting, 19, 71–73, **72**

in-laws, 42–43, 81
insect beings, 11

jewelry, 41, **59**, 60–61, **61**, 73–75

Kinaalda ceremony, 15, 49
Klah, Hosteen, 116–117

land, 17, 21, 25, 27
language, 10, 17, 104–107
laws, 97–98
leaders, 30–33
leases, mining and drilling, 98–99
Lewis, Roger Abel, **76–77**
life cycle, 38, 46–52, 52
livestock, 20, **31**, 33, 43, 62, 94, **98–99**, 108–109
livestock reduction, 97, **98–99**
Long Walk, The, 92, **93**, 117
looms, **44–45, 64**

Manuelito, 91, **91**, 118
maps, **18, 93**
marriage, 30, 49–51
marriage ceremony, 68
matrilineal clans, 30
meat, 20, 33, 71, 94
medicine, 53
medicine man, 34, **50**, 51, 83
men, work of, 19, 41, 53–54, 71–75
Mexican clothing, 60
migration, 17, 53–54mining, 98
missionaries, 19, 33, 95–97
Monster Slayer, 15, 80
monsters, 41
Monument Valley, 21, **26–27**, 94, **109**
mountains, 12, 14, 23, 80
Mucho, Ganado, 117

name of Navajo, 19

Narbona, 90
Navajo Nation, 119
Navajo Tribal Code, 108
Navajo Tribal Council, 98–99
New Mexico, 17, 21, 90, 91–92, 102
newlyweds, 42

oil, 98–99
origins, 17–19. *See also* creation story

Painted Desert, 21–22
poetry, 118–119
population, 102
pottery, 20, 68
prayers, 12, 15, 27, 34, 85, 117
puberty, 49
Pueblo Indians, 19, 20, **20**, 30, 33, 54, **59**, 60, 65, 90

ramadas, 26, **31**, **40**, 41–42
rawhide, 58–60
recipe, 57
religion, 78–87, 86–87
reservations, **18**, 92–94, 94, **95**, 102, 104, **109**, 114, 118
rites and rituals, 49, 81, **81**, 82, 117. *See also* ceremonies
rugs, 20, 62–63, **63**, 94, 117

sandpaintings. *See* drypaintings
schools, **96**, 97
sewing, 58–60, 60
shades. *See* ramadas
sheep, 26, 33, **32**, 43, 62, 94, 97, **98–99**, 108–109
silverwork, 73–75, **7 4**, 94
sings, 80, 83, 85
Smith, Red, 75, 115
songs, 21, 47, 70, 82
Spanish conquest, 90
Spanish influence, 19, 20, 30, 33, **59**, 60–62, 73
Spider People, 12
Spider Woman, 15, 66–68

Squaw Dance ceremony, **7 9**
stories, 10, 66–68. *See also* creation story
storytelling, 17
summer, 42, 54–55, 64
supernatural beings, 10
"surround" hunting, 73
sweat lodges, 14, 42

taboos, 17, 81
tanning hides, 58–60
Tapahonso, Luci, 118–119, **118**
territory, **18**, 21–27
time line, 112–113
tools, 19, 58, 75
trading posts, 94–95, **9 5**, 108
transportation, **88–89**
treaties, 75, 90, 92, 95, 102, 114, 117, 118
twins, 15, 82

vocabulary, 106–107

warfare, 71–73, 90–92
warriors, 19, 90
weapons, 19, 71–73
weaving, 20, 43, **44–45**, 62–66, **65**, 67–68, 94, 117
websites, 123
wedding baskets, **69**
wedding ceremony, 51
White World, 14
winter, 39–41, 64
women, work of, 19, 26–27, 41, 53–55, **56**, 58–60, 62–64, 108–109
wool, 20, 62–63, 94
work, 30, 68–70
Worlds of Creation, 10–17, 80

yarn, **64**
Yeibichai ceremony, 49, 116–117
Yellow World, 12

Zah, Peterson, 119, **119**

Raymond Bial

HAS PUBLISHED OVER THIRTY CRITICALLY ACCLAIMED BOOKS OF PHOTOGRAPHS for children and adults. His photo-essays for children include *Corn Belt Harvest, Amish Home, Frontier Home, Shaker Home, The Underground Railroad, Portrait of a Farm Family, With Needle and Thread: A Book About Quilts, Mist Over the Mountains: Appalachia and Its People, Cajun Home,* and *Where Lincoln Walked.*

He is currently immersed in writing *Lifeways*, a series of books about Native Americans. As with his other work, Bial's deep feeling for his subjects is evident in both the text and illustrations. He travels to tribal cultural centers, photographing homes, artifacts, and surroundings and learning firsthand about the lifeways of each of these peoples.

A full-time library director at a small college in Champaign, Illinois, he lives with his wife and three children in nearby Urbana.